LETTERS TO KAREN

LETTERS
TO
KAREN

On Keeping Love in Marriage

Charlie W. Shedd

ABINGDON • Nashville

To Vincent

our wise young son-in-law
who seems to sense that
the surest way to be fully loved
is to love fully

Preface

This is for Karen. She is one of the fair young daughters of Eve who grace our land. Karen is many things. She is chiefly a lover of peace. But for combat she is armed with cunning. (She has four brothers.) In jeans and sweat shirt she has all the charm of the girl next door. Then again, dressed for the ball, she bears herself with elegance. At times she is somewhat of a romp. Yet on other occasions she would go with you to the deepest interiors.

Ardent and adorable, comely and clever, winsome and wise—that's Karen!

I'm her dad. I know what you're thinking, and you are right. There are *some* prejudiced fathers. But if you knew Karen as I know Karen, you would say, "Now speakest thou the truth plainly!"

Several months before she was married, Karen asked me to write her some special letters. "Daddy," she said at her beaming best, "I'd like you to tell me how I can keep him loving me forever!"

There are two reasons why my daughter would make such a request. For one thing, I am a pastor. As such, I have discussed matrimonial matters with countless couples. I have also spent many hours with wives alone and husbands by themselves.

This is nothing unusual these days. Most of my clergymen friends are caught up in the marriage entanglements of their people.

What can we do?

Sometimes very little. This is especially true when their minds are already set. They come for agreement, not advice. Occasionally one wants to negotiate, but the other will not.

So we can only watch in horror while another home crashes on the hard rocks of charges, counter-charges, bitterness, and revenge.

As you would do, we try to lend a hand in picking up the pieces. This is especially difficult if there are children. They may remind us of broken eggs whose nests have been blown from beneath them.

Then we have our good days when everything goes well. Frequently, this is not our doing. We sense a mysterious visitation, some "holy hunch," which could only come from wisdom greater than our own.

Now we may witness one of the pastor's big thrills. The quarrelers kiss and make up. "Chords which were broken will vibrate once more."

That's how it is. Bewilderment to keep us wondering!

Failure to keep us humble! Success to keep us trying! So, anymore, as they come through my study door I join the Brittany fishermen in their winsome prayer, "Keep us, O God! The sea is so big and our boats are so little!"

You will agree it was a reasonable request which my daughter made. Certain rules apply to every marriage. Yet each wedding also creates a pattern which will develop its own unique involvements.

Accordingly, these letters left my mailbox with a father's prayer that they might be useful to one woman and her beloved.

But most of us need every possible aid for better fulfilling the laws of love. We need help in learning the language of devotion.

Because this is true, these letters are offered here with the added wish that they may be helpful to others—young, mature, older—as they accept this challenge.

Is there any greater hope than this? If we *can* succeed in building happier homes, we have the satisfaction of knowing that we have helped this much to create a healthy society.

I said there were two reasons why my particular daughter might ask me to write some answers to her question. As I was saying, she is an astute young lady. She knows how little her dad really knows. But she also knows another thing.

Reason two is the subject of letter one.

CHARLIE W. SHEDD

Contents

Marriage . . . .

is not so much *finding* the right person
as it is *being* the right person!

"EXHIBIT A"

My dear Karen,

You always were a clever little thing, and I see you have lost none of your touch.

They say, "Flattery will get you everywhere!" It did this time. You sent me quickly to my typewriter. Wouldn't any father swell with pride before such admiration? Imagine that! *My* daughter thinks that much of *my* opinions.

But when I sat down to begin, a great light dawned!

Your request *is* a superb compliment, but it is not for me. For twenty years you have been observing "Exhibit A!"

Therefore, brought low once more by your trickery, I accept your proposal as the magnificent bouquet to your mother which it really is.

You know how devoid I am of knowledge in many areas. But you also know that on one item I *am* an unmitigated authority. Firsthand, I understand how good it is to be loved by a genius in the art of being a wife.

It will be fun describing my favorite person, so I'll be writing you again real soon.

Love,
Dad

WE KNOW IN PART

My dear Karen,

      When you were in high school you went with many boys. We watched on tiptoe when some new date came to the house. Would this be *the* one?

If my memory serves me correctly, not one of them was a total collapse. We admired your taste. They were all nice-looking. Even the big clown who was "so homely he's cute," as you put it, wasn't overly hard on our eyes.

We liked something about every boy you ever dated.

(Come to think of it, there was that one you said reminded you of "a stray puppy looking for a home." We thought he'd never go away. He was the nearest to an exception.)

We would discuss them between us, your mother and I, and we were proud of your friends. They were well-

17

mannered, clean-cut, nicely groomed when they should be, and "such good drivers." This last is what you told us, and I guess you are living proof of your claim.

That giant he-man football player took our eye. He must have spent a fortune calling you long-distance. He reminded us of a Saint Bernard dog—huge, but so gentle and leisurely.

Then came a night I'll never forget. It was after you had dated him for some time. I was still up when you came in, and you announced that you had just crossed him off your list, too. You know how it is with fathers. I was afraid that something unpleasant had happened.

"No," you assured me, "he's so sweet. But, Daddy, could we visit a little right now?"

As nearly as I can recall them your exact words were: "I worry sometimes about me. It seems as if all the boys I ever go with are just darling for a while and then I get bored. After a few dates it's as if I know all there is to know. Do you think there's something wrong with me? I'm scared when I think about getting married. How could I possibly spend my whole life with one man? Do you suppose I'll ever find one interesting enough to keep my attention forever?"

Of course I assured you that someday one would appear, riding from out of somewhere, and he would have ample soul to keep you entertained for always. You said you weren't sure I was right. Then you made this speech which rang the deep bells in my heart.

You took me by the hand and said, "Daddy, I made a big decision tonight. I'm never, ever going to get married unless I meet a boy who is so great it will take a whole lifetime to know everything there is about him."

I thought this was terrific. That night you reached out and touched the pulse of your future husband.

Time passed and suddenly your question marks stood erect like exclamation points! ! !

The first we knew of this was one evening about supper time. You called from the university, do you remember? There was a delightful new awe in your voice. You said, "Daddy, there is this perfectly fabulous boy who waits tables in our dorm. He's the most interesting person I've ever met. He's been around the world so many times." (That's what you said, but I guess it's only twice, isn't it? Can a fellow make it more often than that in the Navy unless he's a career man?)

Like a lovely brook you babbled on, "He knows so much more than I do about everything. And is he ever smart! He understands all about television. That's his major. And he's practically an authority on Latin America. That's his other major. Oh, yes, I forgot to tell you his name is Vincent! Isn't that the most beautiful name? He's worked his way through school and done more things. Besides, he's handsome, and you never saw anybody who understands people like he does. Everybody just loves him because he can talk about any subject they bring up.

"And, Daddy, you know how crazy you and Mother were about Greece? Well, he knows everything about Greece. His ship was stationed there for three weeks."

And so on, and so on, and so on.

I recall clearly that you had me so much in orbit with you I even temporarily forgot this was a collect call. It

19

flashed through my mind that I'd have to ask my friend Jim (he's division manager of the telephone company) if there might be special rates for historical occasions.

Then you threw another bunch of stars at me and away we went once more. Finally, I came back to earth again, and it occurred to me that people in the parish do have emergencies and we'd better open the phone lines at some future date, just in case.

Finally, we agreed that as soon as he could get time off from his many jobs he should drive you home in his dreamy little Volkswagen and let the whole family see for themselves.

"What was *that* all about?" one of your brothers asked when I hung up. "That," I announced, "was about Karen's future husband!" "Her *what?*" they shouted in unison, and we really had ourselves a family pow-wow that night.

Then you brought him home, and we saw what you meant. Here was the dream man your heart was calling to that evening as we sat discussing those tremendous things together.

One of the greatest things ever written on love is I Corinthians 13. The next time you read it, notice that the only repetition in the entire chapter is this:

"We know in part!"

The writer seems to be saying, "Back up and have one more look at the endless vistas of love. Here is something you must consider again. Beauty in human relations does not require total knowledge all at once."

We can be everlastingly thankful for this in many ways. For one thing, am I ever glad people can't see all the way through me! Then, when we go back and review it again, isn't it also fine that we don't know all about other people? If it weren't for this double protection we'd probably all join in that crazy chorus, "Stop the world, I want to get off!"

But when it applies to marriage, this is nothing less than a stupendous gift. To be married to someone in whom you see islands to be discovered, mountains to climb, valleys to explore, and new wonders beckoning off in the distance—this *is* absolutely the greatest.

It does create some problems though. You can't learn how to handle people such as this all at once. It's true the days will never grow dull if you once begin this journey. Yet, on the other hand, it may also be exasperating sometimes.

So when you feel like saying, "Men! Why *does* my husband do such crazy things? Will I ever understand what makes him act like that?"—when you feel this way, you just be grateful for a man you *can't* comprehend all at once.

This beauty of a partial knowledge is what makes life with your loved ones so fascinating. It could exhaust you if you let it. But it can also keep your heart singing with the thrill of just being alive.

Your mother and I have been married twenty-six years, and—this is the truth—new thrills come fresh from her soul every day. I'm still finding out things about her I never knew before—still thankful for someone so tremendous it will take me a lifetime to search her out fully —still glad of heart the whole day long that "we know in part."

You will remember Aletha. She helped us take care of

you when you were little. She worked part-time, but she left a full-time imprint. We came to be the kind of friends where you don't worry what you say around each other. That is why, when we became a bit parent-cross or if we spoke too harshly to one of you, she would gather you up in her arms and say, "Aw, now! All they needs is a great big bunch of waitin' on the Lord!"

That's a great word for parenthood. It also works magic for a man and woman seeking to blend two lives together.

Don't push too hard! Pray for patience! Give each other room to grow!

Listen! Do you hear what I hear? It's a distant sound and deep, like a drummer drumming. I hope you like it. We'll hear him often at his theme as we go along together, and these are the words which fit the beat:

Marriage is not a ceremony! This is a creation!

Yours for joy in the vast unknown,
Dad

HAPPINESS IS TO GROW UP

My dear Karen,

Many couples make the mistake of thinking that two saying "I do!" means "We did it!" They assume that by the mere act of climbing the chancel steps they have already vaulted the stairs into seventh heaven.

Some sociologists say this originates with the Hollywood moonglow in our movies and television. Others blame the romantic writers. Or is it the fault of the songmakers?

Right now, tracing the source is not so important as a full understanding of this fact:

Marriage may be "made in heaven" in the original. But the whole deal is more like one of those kits which comes knocked down for putting together. It will take some gluing here, sanding rough spots there, hammering a bit now, filing down the scratches on this side, planing a bit on that side, carving a piece, bending this section slightly, varnishing, backing off for a frequent look, dusting, waxing, polishing, until at last what you have is a thing of beauty and a joy forever.

If you will look in the "H" section of your American College Dictionary, you will find these important words: *"Happiness results from . . . attainment of what one considers good. . . . Contentment is a peaceful kind of happiness in which one rests without desires, even though every wish may not have been gratified."*

These words apply to even the best unions. Marriage does not suddenly make imperfect people perfect. Every human being has some flaws. This sweeping statement, I regret to inform you, *does* include Vincent. It also includes you.

Handling such a challenge is largely a matter of mature thinking. Every one of us at some earlier date has been in love with the "dream image" of what our perfect lover would one day be. If either of you insists on clinging to your fantasy unduly, you may be in for some real disappointments.

I recall one young bride who returned from her honeymoon quite upset. She had married a much older man. We all thought it might be a good match under their particular set of circumstances. But she came to me considerably shaken. She said she simply hadn't been able to recover from the first night when he took out his teeth and put them in a glass on the hotel dresser. He insisted on a soft light during their lovemaking. But those

24

infernal choppers leering at her from the glass cut her response to nil. She knew he had false teeth. But she had never inquired what he did with them at night!

Thank goodness, most of the cruel blows which shatter our "ideal mate" are not quite that garish. But they will come. So it is important that you "put away childish things." One such is whatever may be left of the phantom heroes of your girlhood.

If you hang on too tightly you may risk a couple of serious errors. You could waste a good deal of time and energy trying to make your man over into something he was never meant to be. You might also be concentrating so much on *what he is not* that you become blind to some of the fine things which make him what he is.

With almost everyone whom we learn to know well, we discover that certain defects are part of the price they pay for their virtues. An attractive person is not so much a collection of miscellaneous parts, good and bad, strewn about. What makes him appealing is more likely to be the way in which he has organized those parts.

The same thing goes for homemaking. In a vital marital combination two wise persons are trying to organize their parts into oneness which will be good for both of them. To see each other work on this, to help each other accomplish this, is one of the dynamics of marriage at its best.

So don't let glamor victimize you. You are not flawless yourself, and you'd be very uncomfortable if Vincent should prove the first exception to this rule—boys have blemishes and young men come unfinished to the wedding.

Take an honest look at his faults. Look in the mirror at your own weaknesses. Then study how you can fit your two sets of faults into your two sets of strong points to make the best blending possible.

When you marry, you become more vulnerable to disappointment and hurt than you have ever been before. But you have decided it is worth the risk.

You have chosen wisely. Only by taking this chance can you become eligible for the bliss which is two people "oneing" themselves together.

There is an anonymous essay in my files which is a favorite of ours. It is written by a ten-year-old boy named Tommy for his school composition. There are two words here which stand out in bold relief against the background of future happiness. This is his theme:

What Is Love?

Love is something that makes two people think they are pretty even when nobody else does. It also makes them sit close together on a bench even when there's plenty of room. It's something which makes two people very quiet when you are around. And when they think you're gone they talk about roses and dreams. And that's all I know about love until I grow up!

Let's hope he's one of the fortunate who learns that love grows finer if you find someone with whom you can share these two key words:

"*Grow up!*"

Good for Tommy! Good also for Karen and Vincent and

every one of us faced with the challenge of bringing roses and dreams to reality behind our own doors.

We like to believe that you are both mature for your age. But never forget that maturity is in part knowing where you need to become more mature.

We have heard you say, "Vincent and I are terribly in love." Whether your love is terribly terrific or terribly terrible may depend sometimes on Tommy's two words: *"Grow up!"*

Best wishes for a maturing love,

Dad

LET FREEDOM RING

My dear Karen,

   "Divine Wedlock" is an ecclesiastical term which has a nice solid ring wherever you hear it. In two words it seems to bring together that hallowed security which just about everybody hopes to find someday.

But you do well to understand that this is never right unless there are two keys to the lock. You are each entitled to one of these, and they are yours to use in wisdom.

"Everything I Have Is Yours!" "You Can Have Me if You Want Me, but You Must Be Mine Alone!" "Why Not Take All of Me?"—this sort of thing may go well in the slushy songs of the sentimentalists. But marriage at its best does not live by the code of the jukebox. It lives by the gradual integration of two people who give each other plenty of room for personal development.

28

Like so many other things in husband-wife relationships, there is a fine line here. Because each marriage represents the bringing together of two unique persons, no one can tell exactly where the "liberty line" is best marked off in your union. It will take careful testing and stretching to find yours together.

Right now I am working with a young wife who was on the receiving end of a big shock recently. Her husband announced that he wanted one night out each week, and, in addition, he did not expect to report where he had been. He simply put his request calmly and told her he would give her some time to think it over.

This was particularly hard for Sally. They had been married less than six months, and she grew up with the idea that "when you marry you tell each other everything."

But this is an astute young lady. She agreed to think it over and sought help for the right answer. As we discussed it, she began looking for clues in his background.

Here is an excellent starting place when someone has hurt you. You know that others often do odd things *to* you for reasons which did not originate *with* you. They may be "working through" a childhood repression, "surfacing" some old conflict, or struggling again with a problem which began long before you knew each other.

A wholesome sympathy based on understanding often has a clarifying effect on both of you. If you can keep the tears out of your eyes long enough, you may be able to "see" where he is blind. And if you learn to project your "love-light" carefully, you may contribute to his own "self-transparency." So, whenever you are wounded, try

29

to begin at the point of saying, "Perhaps this is *his* problem. Before I let it become mine, let's see if it can be an occasion for our maturing together."

This is true bigness, isn't it? It requires a high level of maturity to "act" in love rather than to "react" with hostility.

Thank goodness Sally was big enough to take her mind off her own wounds and focus on his. She knew that Jeff was the youngest of several children. There had never been the privacy in his home which she was allowed in hers. He was not permitted the precious little secrets of childhood. His parents were making decisions for him long after he should have been making them for himself. In his teens he was subjected to an inquisition following every date. She also knew that his father was basically distrustful of everyone, including members of his own family.

As she talked about the problem, she considered several possibilities. She toyed with the idea of retaliation. She might ask for one night out in seven on *her* own with no accounting. But she decided this was not her best move.

"At first," she said, "this might keep him home but it wouldn't solve the problem. He needs to think that someone has complete faith in him. Besides," she admitted, "a night out by myself would be a bore to me!"

Then she made a statement which I wrote down after she left. You might like to memorize this:

"I decided," she concluded, "that maybe *it would be smart if I let him think I am all his and he is all his own!*"

That is a remarkable observation for one in the tender first year of marriage, don't you think?

So, she granted him his request. One exciting night out each week with no reporting to anyone.

This has been going on for three months now and guess what's happening! Jeff is spending more and more of those "free nights" at home or taking her out. Her secret formula is doing its job so well that he even volunteered last week to tell her where he had been going. Every one of those evenings by himself he had either been to a movie alone or shooting billiards with the boys. That's what he said, and I believe him.

You can see that Sally, by her feminine prudence, has led him to the sense of freedom which he needs. But, unknown to himself, she is actually drawing him closer to herself. You sense, of course, that the next step up in their marriage will come when he catches on and begins to be equally wise in handling her.

I see some men who never get the message. They operate under the delusion that a successful husband is one who imprisons "the little woman" within the prison of *his* desires.

Some women give in to this treatment and resign their individuality. But this is not living, and it is never marriage at its best. "Togetherness" isn't always healthy. It may be what my psychiatrist friends call "symbiotic." In everyday language this means that two different kinds of emotional illness have come together in a manner which supports them both for a period, or perhaps for a lifetime.

This is not for folks such as you. No wife is in her right place if she is crushed under the total domination of a tyrant husband. You will recognize at once that the same thing applies vice versa.

So, I hope you'll both remember this interesting paradox about "togetherness." It must include whatever amount of "apartness" is right for each of you. And if you allow plenty of room for the "apartness," this has a way of magnetizing the "togetherness."

In other words, the more you can be free *from* each other without resentment when you feel the need for freedom, the more you will be free *with* each other in sharing your full selves.

Some of the best psychologists I know tell me that mental health depends in large measure on a person's ability to discover his real self and disclose it to at least one other person. Wise couples accept this and begin building these two-way streets early in their marriage.

In our last letter we talked about "growing up." In another we'll discuss "growing outward." We will also consider "going out together." Here let's note that some "going out alone" may be good stuff for the first layers of that healthy escape route which may circle around to bring you closer to each other in the end.

Down this road you should permit each other to go some places where you keep up special interests which appeal to you alone. You can have friends which are your very own, and he can have some which are his. Certain matters which seem like trivia to you may be very important to him. The same is true from your side. (Of course, all this can be overdone, and some couples overdo it.) But mature mates will leave off their cooing long enough to provide whatever freedom is essential for developing their individuality as they develop their oneness.

This mutual independence is actually a large part of

your heritage. Your background in home, church, school, and nation has provided you with the cardinal concepts of this great way of life.

Therefore, seek to make your dwelling place a little republic, inhabited first by two citizens, later by others, each with sacred rights and privileges of his own. Don't overinvade each other's privacy. Don't hold on so tight that you squeeze one another away.

This is a big order for a woman who loves her man so much that she wants to share everything with him all at once. You love Vincent that much. You want to be "all his" and long for him to be "all yours." We know he feels the same toward you.

But I've got news for you—you will only reach the sublime heights of perfect union if you pledge each other freedom enough to develop the original creation which is the "high, holy place" in each individual.

This is Divine Wedlock—two people growing both individually and in unity until they become what they were meant to be together.

Let freedom ring,
Dad

YOURS FOR FUN

My dear Karen,

   Thought you might enjoy something from your own family background.

In musing on the imperfections which turn up in our "perfect" sweethearts after the wedding I remembered this one.

When we were first married your mother couldn't abide my habit of leaving the dresser drawers open. But I honestly thought this is how it was supposed to be. A man wants a shirt? So he makes his selection from the top drawer and leaves the drawer open. He needs socks? Make the choice from drawer three and leave it open.

I'm telling you the truth—I thought that closing drawers was one reason God created women. My mother had been closing dresser drawers behind me for twenty-two years.

34

But in less than twenty-two hours I discovered that my new bride simply couldn't tolerate this utter thoughtlessness.

I am almost embarrassed to tell you what sent me into tantrums in her behavior. I discovered to my horror that this beautiful creature I was tied to forever had a horrendous habit—*she squeezed the toothpaste tube in the middle rather than carefully rolling it from the bottom!* (You see right here that there are some things you might not find out about your "intended" before marriage.)

Why did she do this awful thing? Because she had always squeezed it that way. Her family couldn't care less about toothpaste tubes.

But they did care about drawers. For them, closing drawers was a symbol of things done decently and in order. It also had another meaning. It signified that each member of the household was being considerate of every other member.

Of course, it all seems silly now. This, incidentally, is another of the nice things life has a way of doing for us. It makes things look funny from a distance which were anything but that close up.

I hope you'll have a million laughs as you open up the clown-rooms inside yourselves.

Yours for fun,
Dad

EMPHASIS ON
THE GOOD THINGS

My dear Karen,

High on the list of happy marriages which your mother and I have known is the union between Bob and Helen J.

On the surface they seem to have little in common. Bob is a pusher and she is retiring. He is the life of the party. You'll usually find her in the shadows. But they are radiantly in love.

We noticed it first at a banquet while some visiting speaker was giving his address. Part of the time they held hands. Now and then they looked at each other with a sly smile, as if they were reading loud and clear some silent message between them.

Then one night we were invited to dinner at their

house. You would have loved it. He went to the kitchen a couple of times, and I heard him ask if there was anything he could do. Once she said, "No thanks, honey. Take it easy!" The next time she let him pour the water.

When we went to the table he held her chair and then, of all things, he *served her first!* I don't know what the etiquette books say about this, but my guess is it wouldn't have shamed him one bit. And she didn't protest. She sat there glowing as if this were the way to do things and wasn't life wonderful?

It was.

The whole dinner was a thing of beauty. Several times in the conversation he asked her opinion on some subject and even listened while she told what she thought about it. When the meal was finished, he rose to help her clear the table.

After dinner, while he and I were alone in the den, I decided to find out more about this. "Bob," I said, "you and Helen seem so perfectly adjusted to each other. I've watched you for some time now, and I think it's great. I see so many unhappy marriages. Do you have any secrets I might pass on to others?

He laughed a bit but more in hesitation than embarrassment. In a few moments he recited a story which I think is a classic.

"We had a terrible time when we were first married," he began. "In fact, we even talked about calling it quits. Then we read something that gave us an idea. We decided to make a list of all the things we didn't like about each other. Of course, it was hard, but Helen gave me hers and I gave her mine. It was pretty rough reading. Some of

37

the things we had never said out loud or shared in any way.

"Next, we did something which might seem foolish so I hope you won't laugh. We went out to the trash basket in the backyard and burned those two lists of bad things. We watched them go up in smoke and put our arms around each other for the first time in a long while.

"Then we went back into the house and made a list of all the good things we could dig up about each other. This took some time, since we were pretty down on our marriage. But we kept at it and when we finished we did another thing which might look silly. Come on back to the bedroom and I'll show you."

It was a neat room, lots of light, and a happy spread on the big old bed from grandma's house.

But at the focal point in that bedroom wall there were two plain maple frames, and in them what do you suppose?

In one was the list of the good things Helen could see in Bob. In the other was his scribbled list of her virtues. That's all there was. Just two scratchy lists behind glass.

"If we have any secret," Bob continued, "I guess this is it. We agreed to read these things at least once a day. Of course, we know them by heart now. I couldn't begin to tell you what they've done for me. I recite them to myself sometimes when I'm driving the car or waiting for a customer. When I hear fellows complain about their wives I think of my list and thank my lucky stars. Funny, too, the more I consider the good she sees in me the more I try to be like that. And when I really understood her good points I tried all the harder to build on these. Now I think she's the most wonderful person in the world. I guess she sort of likes me too. That's all there is to it!"

That's *all*, the man says!

But it goes right to the heart of great marriage. This kind of love has a way of gradually canceling out the bad and raising up the good.

You'll be interested to know that I have suggested Bob and Helen's technique many times in marriage counseling. I've seen it work real miracles. Sometimes they had simply forgotten the great thoughts they held for each other before the ring exchange. Usually these things slip away on padded feet. Before we know it the affirmative has disappeared and our thoughts are slanted in the direction of "She's all right *but*" or "He'd be so much nicer *if only!*"

Of course, you must face up to the negatives, and we'll get to this later. But you will be more attractive to each other in the home, you will learn to appreciate the good in others outside your walls, and they will more readily recognize the best in you if you slant your marriage in this direction.

Here is another word from I Corinthians 13 which is worth weaving into the fabric of your thoughts: *"Love does not rejoice at wrong but rejoices in the right."*

Positively,
Dad

TELL HIM HE'S WONDERFUL

My dear Karen,

Have I ever told you about the little girl's essay on "What Makes a Marriage Great?" She wrote, "I guess it's when you love each other the right way, or enough, or something. I think to make a marriage great you have to treat each other like company a lot of the time and be polite and stuff like that!"

While couples are courting, they usually give considerable thought to ways and means of pleasing each other. "What can I do to make him happy?" and "I wonder if she would like this?" are common questions on the wooer's list.

It is a wise couple who continues this expression of their love into marriage and even increase it as the years pass. I'm not contending for words alone. Sometimes by your actions you can "speak" the depths of your feeling. A silent bit of tenderness well done at the right time may get your message through every bit as much as if you had said it out loud.

But a whole host of husbands and wives never approach the maximum. Three sad words describe many a marriage—"They quit courting." Sometimes this happens all at once. More likely it leaves the place gradually as they begin to take each other for granted.

Let me tell you about an experiment which I conducted recently. (I hate to do this because it shows us men up as the clods we really are, but let's face it!) One Sunday morning I left the pulpit early, turned the closing moments over to our associate pastor, and slipped up to the custodian's second-floor closet. His window overlooks the parking lot, and I wanted to watch the congregation leaving for home.

What I was about was to count the gentlemen-husbands who still open the car door for their wives.

It is safe to assume that ten out of ten did this little extra during their pre-marriage dating. But behold how the vision splendid fades!

The sad statistics are these: Only *three husbands in every ten* made their way to the opposite side of their automobiles to assist their ladies aboard. For seven out of ten it was as though by marrying these strong noblemen they had gained enough strength to open the car door for themselves!

These are all nice people, you understand, but they have fallen into that common error of those three sad words: "They quit courting!"

Important question here: *Will your marriage see an increase or a decrease in the little chivalries which make all the difference between a continuing romance and just another marriage?* Your answer may depend on the little girl's all-important directive—"be polite and stuff like that!"

Yet this emphasis on "doing" is not meant to minimize the importance of well-chosen words sincerely spoken at strategic times. This is one of the least expensive ingredients in the great marriages I have known. But it too does a steady fadeaway unless you consciously cultivate it daily.

If you were to knock on every door in any block and ask how long it has been since hubby complimented wife, or vice versa, you might be surprised. The truth is that many married couples seem to have a filter on their lips preventing the passage of a kind word. Yet here is something which costs nothing, makes life more bearable, and sets the heart singing.

One night at a men's meeting, with you in mind, I asked those in attendance to write a few words on the subject, "What My Wife's Compliments Mean to Me."

Here are a few excerpts selected from more than forty statements:

> "Compliments? You bet! Like this writer guy I read puts it, 'I bring home the bacon and she furnishes the applesauce.'"

> "I think complimenting each other is one of the most important things in marriage. Whenever she praises me I feel as if she is pouring a larger mold. I have to grow bigger to fill it."

"My wife is my most ardent fan and my best press agent."

Nice, aren't they? May it ever be so with you. But perhaps to give the full picture, I should add some which must have come from barren hearts. (I asked them not to sign their names.)

"I run a store and my wife reminds me of those women who come stomping down the aisles looking for the manager."

"My wife never compliments me. I feel sometimes like saying, 'Oh, for gosh sakes, quit your harping and go get a horn.'"

"There is one man in our club whose wife is always praising her husband. I wish I had a woman like that. My wife doesn't know any compliments. She's on a constant safari looking for my faults."

"These are they which come out of great tribulation" and may it never be so for Vincent. Remember, my darling daughter, you can keep him loving you forever if you learn a thousand different ways to tell him he's wonderful.

But you better learn how to do this right. There are some important points to keep in mind.

For one thing, if you come at it nicely, *appreciation can be the background for showing him his faults.* Every couple in marriage should be growing toward personal betterment on both sides, or their union is stuck on dead center. We'll be seeing more of this when we discuss the art of disagreement and telling the truth in love. But right here it's enough to remember that varnish always melts under heat. You can only tell him he isn't wonderful where he isn't if you have told him he is wonderful where he is.

You will also be wise to *watch for signs that you aren't giving him adequate nourishment for his ego.* Most husbands now and then overpraise themselves. When yours does this too much, it may mean that he needs more of your praise. Watch for it also when you are with others. If he pushes the crowd away from the footlights and demands top billing for himself, this may be your fault. Come out of the balcony and move to the front row.

Another indicator is oversensitivity. Whenever he is ultradefensive of his own prestige, when his happiness depends entirely on the nod of a head outside your walls, you're not slipping—you've slipped.

Comes now another cue for the clever wife. *Every man has certain areas where he's particularly pleased if his woman applauds.* This can be a secret little game you play between you. If you play it well, he may grow beyond it until he doesn't need it any more. But it will be important at the outset because most every man is not as good as he would like to be at some points. Your mother was an ace at this in our early days together. As you know, I played football, baseball, basketball, and nearly every game with a ball in it. Because I was big, I got by rather well at some of these. But the truth is that I was lazy.

As I look back over the gridirons and diamonds and courts where I played, I was never as good as I would like to have been. But there *was* one spot where I was a walloping success. (Well, anyway, for a time I was!) This was in wrestling. As you know, I still hold a title back in my home state. So, what if it is the record for being thrown quicker than anyone else in the heavyweight finals? I loved wrestling, and I was right there in the thick of it. Then I met my match, and Goliath went down with a resounding thud.

Yet, you'd never have known all this from your mother. She guarded my secret until I was grown up enough to tell it myself. She skillfully cast my praises about. Then, as your husband will, her husband made it over the hump. He decided to come clean. Yours, too, will have these places of pride and places of shame. You will do well to learn them and play to the gallery. It may take time, but, as the years are sure to pass anyway, you can both have fun with this diversion. Wise wives are like that.

But having rid ourselves of this bit of chicanery, let's transfer the thought to the thing which counts most. When love is done playing, when it reaches its best, *sincerity is an absolute must for the phrases of praise.*

Some atomizerlike women go giddily spraying their vapors all over the place. Yet, though men may appear to enjoy it, most males want more than chattery flattery from the women they love. (I like this apt phrase making the rounds of our high school gang these days: "Take the roof off the greenhouse, mother! The corn is getting taller!")

So be sure your words have the feel of the real. He needs the authentic from you.

The postman is due. But before I seal the envelope, let's roll them over our tongues once more: "I think you're wonderful!"

If ever one sentence weighed a ton this is it. I hope Vincent will join your hallelujah chorus. May he sing it often in varied ways. But even if he doesn't, stop longing and begin it yourself. If he is as normal as I think he is, there will be a reaction and it will be good.

Whenever you see a radiant woman, you can be sure she knows she is loved. The same thing goes for men of genuine confidence.

You can bring out the best in each other if you look for the best and put it in words.

With all good wishes for all good praises,
Dad

P. S. There is an old story which supposedly comes from Vermont. They say this old grouch lived with his wife for twenty-one years and never spoke one single word. Then one morning at breakfast he broke the silence with, "Darling, sometimes when I think how much you mean to me it is almost more than I can do to keep from telling you!" (We'll hope it's only a New England folk tale.)

MOODS! MOODS! MOODS!

My dear Karen,

Last night before you left for school you asked me, "Can't I do something about these awful moods?" You said Vincent was "down in the dumps," and I could see you were aching inside.

Let's begin with a fact which you must face: *Moods are a natural part of every personality.* In my experience there are no exceptions among men. (Nor women or children either for that matter.) The only variation to the rule is one of degree or place or time or what motivates the mood. "Sometimes I'm up, sometimes I'm down" is the song of every soul. Even the saints flagged in zeal part of the time.

Come to think of it, isn't this escalator-going-both-ways a part of all life? Music has its somber fugues and gay roundelays. Nature has its cycles. History has its high times and low. It appears that all things fluctuate and husbands are no exception.

Be grateful for the blessings of contrast which these experiences provide. When our loved ones have bad moods, this may make their good stand out in bold relief after the agony has run its course. Perhaps we can appreciate our mates at their best because we are allowed to see them also at their worst.

Maybe you are asking, "But don't moods sometimes move from natural to 'sick'?" They certainly do, and one measurement is the time it takes for emerging. Any moody mind which returns rapidly to the sunshine indicates a healthy climate inside. It is good also to check for frequency. Are the morose moments coming with increasing rapidity? Another evil omen is the roller-coaster pattern —way up one day, way down the next! When these intensify at an alarming rate, you best hurry on down for advice from those who deal daily in troubled minds.

Comes now another item of real importance. *Try your best not to go down into the swamps of despair when he goes down.* This is much easier said than done, of course, and it will take some time to learn this one. It is so easy for you to become melancholy when he becomes melancholy.

Because you love him so much you want to share all things with him fully, and it may appear on the surface that you could help him best by glumming it through together! But "togetherness" of the highest kind does not mean going together to the lowest levels.

If you can keep your heart filled with high-level kindness when he is down, you will really contribute more to his recovery than by almost any other method. This may make him furious at first because most of us have never completely conquered this one subconscious little demon. I refer to the one which can't stand it for others to feel good when we feel bad.

But this initial wrath will pass if you keep calm. When it is over, he will be glad that one pair of feet remains firmly on solid ground. In time, you can work this out to a "deal" where he does his best to stay topside when it is your turn to go below.

One reason why you might be tempted to despondency when he is despondent is that you may blame yourself unduly for his bad moods. If you are at fault and you know it you will say so. But groveling in the emotional sloughs of self-criticism is strictly no good when it is *his* black mood and not your doing. You are growing up when you can honestly say, "I will remember that this is *his* problem. I will refuse to punish myself. My job is to keep calm and ready. I will prepare my heart to give him the most mature love I can manage as soon as he gives me the opening."

I have observed some skillful women doing another clever thing. *They get ready for their husband's bad moods before the low ceiling comes down.*

Maybe you can learn your man's weak points and "seed the tornado" to scatter the ugly winds. One of the most successful wives among our friends says that she asks her husband to barbecue her a steak when she feels some inner woe sneaking up on him. She testifies that the combination of a big meal and her accolades to his cooking works wonders for him.

Maybe you should go dancing. Perhaps a long drive in the moonlight is the right antidote. If he prefers to come home and glower there then put on your best, roll out your dark blue carpet, and let him work it out under his own roof. Some men I know would give their bottom dollar if they could have such a "shelter of a rock from a weary land" in their own home.

If you make enough progress at handling these things together, you might even learn to give each other warning signals. Catherine Anthony says that she and Jim have agreed to this jewel: If he's had a rough day at the office, if he's off his usual cheery base, if the stock market is down, or he lost an account he hoped to get, then Jim wears a red feather in his hat when he comes home. "Warning, dear! This is no evening to present that unexpected bill or to report the broken throttle on the mower!"

There is one thing more you can do. This is, in fact, *the* big curative! It is the one where your mother and I find our most effective remedy. You spell it with four letters: *Talk!*

The phone just rang. It's a couple asking if I can come right now. There are so many husbands and wives who are total strangers to each other in important areas.

So, let's talk about talk in our next letter!

Yours for clearing skies,
Dad

THE BRIDGE
OF COMMUNICATION

My dear Karen,

"Are you good at talking things over? Can
you discuss your feelings together? Are there certain sub-
jects you must tiptoe around? How good are you at com-
municating your inmost thoughts with each other?"

Questions such as these are favorites with premarital
counselors. Most of the couples I marry assure me that
this is one of their strongest points.

But up against their claim put these echoes of common
complaints heard often in our work with couples who
have been married several years.

"You know how you feel when the phone rings
and nobody answers? That's how I feel!"

"Now please don't tell my husband I said that, will you?" . . . "Don't you dare say anything about this to my wife!" . . . "What do you mean, discuss it? My wife is a sphinx!"

"He never answers. He only grunts!" . . . "With us, it's like being married to strangers!"

These are exact quotations from the dirges I've heard, and their variations come often to my ears.

What do you suppose happens to the lovers who were so sure of their ability here? There are many answers, so we'll start with this letter and continue through several more, giving attention to an all-important piece of construction which we will call: *The Bridge of Communication!*

Since sharing your hearts through your lips is basic to marriage at its best, let's begin with three do's and three don'ts which might help you in tending the bridge.

1. *Do greet him with gladness when he first comes home.*
One husband made this picturesque statement: "She throws the garbage in my face first thing when I open the door." Then he went on to explain that she had a knack for saving the worst news of each day and giving him this promptly on his arrival. You will recognize that he was a master with words as he mimicked her patter: "Junior broke the neighbor's bird bath!" . . . "That left rear tire on the station wagon is flat again!" . . . "Won't you *please* fix my kitchen faucet? I told you five days ago how awful it leaks!" . . . "I understand the Watsons are getting a divorce!" . . . and so on in woeful detail.

These evil tidings are strictly no good for his home-coming. Occasionally there must be exceptions, but every good meeting of minds will lay certain items aside for later consideration.

Now, here comes an interesting phenomenon about some men. The same male who objects to this treatment may wish to unload *his* trash the minute he arrives. Maybe he picked up the idea somewhere that wives are for listening to the bad and husbands are for listening to the good.

During your first months together, if he should be one of these, I'd let him get away with it. Obviously, this isn't exactly fair, but be a wise little gal and "play like" that's how you understood it, too.

Turn down the stove if you can, turn the FM to some soothing music, and draw him close. Let your heart be his mourner's bench.

Such gentleness from you in your early days can pave the way for you to teach him later the wisdom of postponing his "Isn't-it-all-just-terrible?" talk.

From what I've seen, it's a good idea to now and then check your words of greeting.

2. Do set aside time for visiting together.

A whimsical cartoon in one of our magazines pictured an attractive mother telling her two children their bedtime story. This was the plaintive caption: "Children, your father is about five-foot-ten, dark hair, cute little mustache, well-tanned, and *he is just wild about golf!*"

Every husband should have his hobby, and the same goes for your side. In one of our early letters we discussed time apart from each other as a magnet which will eventually draw you closer to each other. But the land is full of foolish couples whose love has been diverted now until they are "just wild" about something other than their hours together.

So, what can you do about this? Sometimes little remedies bring big changes. You might add a lot to your way of life by working out what you've heard us call our "conversational compacts."

I'm sure you'll remember what a good thing we did at our house when we all agreed to this pledge: "We will save time for loitering at our evening meal. We will share the day's highlights and discuss these together. We will present our 'most interesting things' and vote on matters important to us all."

In one vital marriage I know, the husband and wife have what they call their "little deal." They say, "It turned out to be one of the biggest deals we ever made!" They promised each other that they would take a few minutes at bedtime to share this question, "What was the happiest moment of your life today?"

Other couples have agreed to at least one meal out together each week. They allow for a baby-sitter in their budget and set aside funds for dinner at one of their favorite eating places. Social events with others do not count. These are their moments alone to "focus their souls."

Of course, there will be extreme emergencies which interrupt any covenant you make. But don't let yourselves go so fast, or be so preoccupied, that you fail to notice the sign approaching this bridge. It reads: "The River of Time!"

3. *Do learn all you can about his work.*

A man came to my study one evening to give me a check. It was a tithe of his first royalty on an invention. How about this for an ideal wife?

"This patent which has begun to pay off," he began, "is really not my idea. Grace studied everything she could find about my work. She read and attended lectures. She talked with every expert she could corner. Then one day she said, 'Al, with your brilliant mind'—that's what she said, you see—'I'll bet you could invent an electronic eye to tell the difference between good peas and bad peas while they're still in the pod. This is how I've got it figured.' "

Then he went on to detail the idea. It was over my head *but it wasn't over his!* He went after it with zeal and developed this ingenious device.

That isn't all the story. Measure the woman now against this additional statement: "She made me promise I would never tell anyone where I got the idea. My bosses think I'm really something. They gave me my own private lab to work up some new money-makers. And guess who's helping me most? How could I ever be grateful enough for a woman like Grace?"

Then he handed me their contribution and asked if I would say a prayer for them. So I prayed. With thanksgiving and praise, I prayed that they might continue to be "in tune" with the Infinite for greater things.

They will! A woman like this is a real find for any man. Let's let that suffice for our third "Do!"

"Don'ts" are important also for the traffic of your heart through your lips. Here are three worth remembering:

1. *Don't let your common interests get away.*

Nearly every couple facing marriage has many things which have drawn them together. But sometimes these die a gradual death from other causes than we have mentioned in our "Do's." What's the reason?

One major origin of this demise is when one member tends to dominate the conversation. Rushing madly from secondly to thirdly to fourthly, they suffocate the dialogue with monologue.

Many of us have this tendency. We love the sound of our own words, and we forget that although our voice may ring like a bell to us, it is more like the caw of a crow to the other person who waits and waits to express himself.

Skillful wives I've known seem to have several marks of wisdom at this point: (a) They know many clever little ways to give their men the "you go first" treatment! (b) They "yield the floor" quickly when they see any indication that he has something to say! (c) They learn how to read their husbands for these signals—the raised eyebrow, the slightest movement in the corner of his lips, a furrowed brow, or some special gesture peculiar to him.

It is true that he should make every effort to be attentive to your thoughts. I hope he'll be as wise about this as he expects you to be. But you'll hear his footsteps on your bridge more often if you develop this delicate radar.

If you do this well, those common interests which meant so much at the beginning can grow through the years. Gradually they become a trellis on which your shared words intertwine. This makes your bridge of communication more attractive to you both.

2. Don't try to impress him with how much you know.

Jealousy of every kind is dangerous stuff in marriage, and one of its worst forms is mental envy. If he knows things unknown to you, you have discovered a great thing when you can humble your mind to say, "I admire your brains! Teach me!"

Then there will be places where your knowledge supercedes his. With this you must be at your best. Without making a display of it, you can learn the technique which we call "putting the latchstring low enough!"

Do you remember when you and Philip were tots we placed a knob on the screen door low enough for you to reach? It saved two youngsters considerable frustration. The idea came from an elderly guest at our house who wearied of your banging for entrance. His suggestion not only made life easier for you, it also saved many steps for mother and dad.

You have observed how many of the truly great people learn to reduce their brilliance to reachable heights. The same goes for both of you. You must each master the art of lowering the handles to give what you do know and to receive what you don't.

Wise wives remember this—he'll take more pride in his woman's discernments if she never parades hers while she plays up his.

3. Don't fail to still your lips when you should.

Actually, this is all we've been saying in our other don'ts, isn't it? We'll probably say it again—and again! The reason for all this repetition is that I see a steady stream of these chattering women as I work with problem marriages.

One group might be labeled "The Interrupters!" This is a common human tendency for many of us. We sit on the edge of our chairs and wait impatiently for an opening. Or sometimes we don't wait! At the first drawing of breath from the other fellow, we seize the floor and tell how it really was or how we know it should be! Since I'm not a lady, I can't tell how it feels from your side, but I have observed that not many of us men go for women who are constantly breaking in on our wisdom.

Another variety of the "ceaseless" might be classified as "Overquestioners!"

The same man who hopes sometime to get in a word, may yearn at other times for nothing more than a peaceful reverie with himself! We all have within us those personal places where our minds are tied in knots, and *we* know the knot is not ready for loosening. Other items require working in private before they can be shaped in correct phrases.

We began our letters on the premise that we do not know everything about each other just because we are married. That concept is worth frequent review.

You *do* have a right to know some things "right this minute!" So does he. But other things will only come across the bridge at their own private pace.

For this reason, to love well is often to wait well.

This could go on and on. But here comes that drummer again! He's sounding his favorite theme—some of the road to heaven must be taken at a slow shuffle!

This is how it is as you develop the art of communication between you. But if you do develop it well, you may come one day to a thrilling experience. This is the great hour when you can commune together in stillness. Marvelous moments these! They need no words. You can drive for miles, sit for long periods, and share your souls in silent conversation. No voice could add to this. All is quiet inside and your hearts are at peace.

Here is a little prayer which I try to remember before every talk and each sermon. It was taught me by a wise professor who knew the value of things said and the worth of the unsaid also. Maybe you'd both like to learn it for your life together:

> *"Lord, fill my mouth with worthwhile stuff*
> *and nudge me when I've said enough!"*

Dad

EYEBALL-TO-EYEBALL

My dear Karen,

"Eyeball-to-eyeball" is the shortened version of what your mother and I call: *"Our seven official rules for a good, clean fight."*

The "oneing" of two hearts calls for much billing and cooing. But if you are wise you will get ready for another sound. This is the battle cry! Wherever two red-blooded people are building a home, you'll find occasional spats and, now and then, some fiery encounter.

This news should not blow you down! If you learn how to handle them, these small wars may be just what your marriage needs.

Venting the air in your insides through lips which have learned how to do it can serve a good purpose in you. It may also be good for other people with whom you associate.

If Vincent has a "blowing-off" place behind his own doors he might be more effective at his work. Most occupations these days require strict sublimation of feelings even when a man has every right to "let himself go." A well-kept skirmish procedure at home can be a blessing to him, a blessing to you, and a blessing to his fellow workers. It could even be a secret to his advancement, and, oh, how we love those raises!

Good, clean fighting can be excellent preventive medicine for your common good health. It might prevent headaches, heartaches, and high blood pressure. Ulcers and allergies, moods and nagging, and a whole host of other things you'd like to avoid can be added to this list.

Besides all this, *it's fun if you do it right!* When some couple says, "We've been married 'X' number of years with never a cross word between us," you should know this—it usually means that they have learned some method of laying their differences on the table and talking them out.

If they really *do* live together with the sheepishness of sheep, then they're missing a lot of real living. In one of our churches, the senior-high president was a cute red-head named Delphine. She was asked to present the lesson one night on an Old Testament character. The "ho-hum" attitude with which she began was not at all like Delphine. But before she was done she summed up her trouble with this classic statement, "Kids, I feel sorry for this man. I've hunted through all his stories, and, as nearly as I can figure it, *the poor guy lived a normal life!*"

I wish I could remember who he was. I can't recall even one well-known Bible character in that sad condition.

Maybe she missed something. But if she was right then we *should* join in her sympathy!

Life is partly for fun, and part of the fun is working out problems, handling differences, struggling for a meeting of minds, surfacing inner entanglements, and learning how to handle these well.

So roll your guns up on the bridge occasionally and get ready for the zip and tang of facing "eyeball-to-eyeball."

Here now are our "Seven Official Rules for a Good, Clean Fight." We signed them in our souls as affirmations, and we'll give them to you here just as we've enjoyed them for twenty-five years.

1. *Before we begin we must* both *agree that the time is right.*

There is an eager little beaver in nearly everyone which likes to get right on with it when something is needling inside. Then we have other days when it takes all our strength just to go on breathing.

A wise woman learns to purr with the kittens sometimes when she would prefer to scratch with the cats. If he's suffering from "battle fatigue" at the office, this is not a good time. The smart man also learns how to command "Arms Rest!" even if his spleen is ready for venting. Since women have hard days with the children and weeks when they're not up to their best, he too must practice self-control. That little word *"both"* in this rule grows more important as you study it.

You can also learn to read each other's signs that the time *is* drawing near for getting on with it. That I might have more expert feminine advice for you, I recently asked a small group of women if they would mind sharing with me their husband's war flags.

Here are four observations which I selected for your musing: "Whenever he begins to swear at the traffic, that's my tip!"—"I can tell something's bothering him when he begins using a whole lot more salt on his food!"—"If he gets unusually fussy about the way his shirts are done, he's getting ready!"—"My man is looking for a fight when he begins complaining about the bills!"

Naturally, these will differ with different men but you can learn Vincent's. Some things better wait. Some things should not wait. Some things might wait too long.

Whatever you do, you *both* better make certain you know the bailiff's two questions, "Is the defendant ready?" and "Is the plaintiff prepared?"

2. *We will remember that our only battle aim is a deeper understanding of each other.*

There are several important gun labels for conversational warfare between husbands and wives who really do care.

"Humility and honesty" will be the theme of a later letter but you'll need these now. Neither of you is "all St. George" and neither of you is "all the dragon."

"Patience" is another requirement. Without it you could tear up more in an hour than it might take weeks to repair.

"Mercy," "Grace," and "Telling the truth in love" should be in your hearts as you shout, "Ready-aim-fire!"

If either of you is to hit the bull's eye you must never forget this: Your main aim is to improve your marriage by deeper understanding!

3. *We will check our weapons often to be sure they're not deadly.*

This follows naturally on the heels of what we've been saying. "The battle unto death" may be all right in its place but its place is not in the home. Here you are shooting down troubles, not firing for funerals!

So be especially careful of the words you hurl when the smoke gets in your eyes.

Right now, I am working to patch up a marriage where they lost their tempers and he made a serious mistake. He shouted in anger, "I *never did* like your darned old freckles anyway!"

She had freckles all over her face, and they were honestly one of the nicest things about her. But they had bothered her since her early teens. He had always told her that he was crazy about them, and I'm sure he was with part of him. But another part was not, and he let that part get out of hand when their fight was at fever pitch.

We're making some progress. He has apologized a thousand times. Yet for a long time there will be that sneaky little worry in her mind, "Does he *really* like my freckles as he has always vowed he did? Or was he telling the truth when he lost control?"

"Sadism" is bad in any form, and one of its worst forms is to throw up to others those things they can *never* change.

Even the mildest criticism is best handed over softly. When it is hurled in rage it may bring retorts which might add nothing and take away much.

We all have within us a defense mechanism which comes roaring out of its corner when we are censored!

Some men learn much from their women about self-control. If you remain master of your tongue, even when he doesn't, he may emerge from this battle with a new respect for a wonderful wife who knows what not to say when!

Another weapon to lay aside permanently is the overused phrases which have become so tiresome that they automatically bring bad reactions. One successful couple I know says that they have agreed to delete "never" and "always" from their battle vocabulary. "You are *never* home on time!" or "You *always* put the children first!" ignite fuses for them which lead to trouble. So they have wisely decided to eliminate these triggering words. You'll soon learn your own "loaded" phrases and do as they've done.

Now comes a paradox! We have said that there are times when no answer is the best answer. But at other times it may be worse *to say nothing* than *to say something!* The utter absence of any utterance from the lady he loves may be one of the loudest noises a man ever heard if he's dying for her to break her silence!

So study rule three and use it smartly. The swords you swing on this "battle of the bridge" must be cut of the stuff which bends and gives. Your cannon balls should be more like snowballs than great balls of fire.

4. *We will lower our voices instead of raising them.*

This is the one rule of our seven which was built into our courtship before we were married. It came, as so many good things of our love, from out of your mother's quiet. In my stormy background we "hollered" when our ire was up, and the volume went higher with the increasing ire.

I have told you how I fell in love with your mother's voice before I had seen her face. She was reciting one day in our high school class. It was a large group of students, and I was staring out the window wondering whether this particular sophomore might start the big game.

Then, like a soft angelus to my ears, came the sound of deep peace. I looked to its source and right then I made a vow. If I ever began to think much of girls, this was the one I'd begin to think much of first.

You know the rest. When we began our dating I sensed what Shakespeare meant when he said, "Her voice was ever soft, gentle, and low, an excellent thing in woman!"

But as with all sweethearts, the first hour of anger arrived, and I began the customary procedure. So she stopped me in my vocal tracks and explained that she knew a better way. "Why don't we agree," she said from her inner stillness, "that from now on when we fuss we'll lower our voices one octave rather than raising them two?"

It's been an awesome struggle. But that's how it is. For a husband to tone down his volume may require the strictest discipline. The same for some women.

5. *We will never quarrel in public nor reveal private matters.*

We belonged to a group in one of our churches which included a pair of bloodhounds. These were "people bloodhounds," a husband-wife pair who were constantly nosing about for each other's negligibles.

Example: He would be reciting the happy memories of their vacation trip. She sniffed along behind him scenting for a mistake. Then it happened. He made *the* horrible error! Recalling the pleasures of their two weeks away he said, "On the first Tuesday it rained, so we stayed in the cabin and played cards!"

Now we go!

"*No! No! No!* Don't you remember, darling, on Tuesday we drove over the mountain. *Wednesday* was the day it rained!"

So the war was on.

"It was *too* Tuesday; it *had* to be Tuesday because, etc., etc.!" Before long we were hearing the full record of Monday, Thursday, Friday, Saturday, Sunday. Then they were marching their soldiers into the second week!

In this group there was a delightfully rugged cattleman whom we called "Big Ed." He was mighty in many ways and one of these was with blasting words when his boilers were going inside. With secret cheers from all of us he roared in their ears, *"Why don't you two do your dirty laundry at home?"*

That is a good question with only one answer. All private rubbing and scrubbing should be done in its place— and its place is in private!

There is one more subpoint to our rule. This is our agreement that we will never fire at each other publicly when we are *not* together. I have known very few men who could readily forgive their wives for criticizing and complaining behind their backs.

Be sure to tell Vincent that women differ little from men right here!

So underscore rule five with a heavy red pencil.

6. *We will discuss an armistice whenever either of us calls "halt."*

Notice the wording, "We will *discuss* an armistice!" Some men are quitters by nature, and some women run up the white flag too soon! With us it requires a unanimous vote of two before we finally sign the truce. Sometimes silence is not golden. It may be a pale shade of yellow.

If you agree to these rules, then a sense of fair play is an absolute must all the way through to the end. Without good sportsmanship on both sides you can't have the kind of "good, clean fight" which our rule-label bears.

Yet, as we have seen, some things in marriage can go either way. Some men want to stay up all night and push the adversary around!

How *can* you end it if you want to quit and he wants to continue? Here is one move for cease-fire which seldom fails for us. It goes like this—"I'm *beginning* to see what you meant! But I'll need some time to think this over. *Please, let's make up now so I can consider awhile how you could be right!*" (He could be, you know!)

If this doesn't get through, your marriage may be sicker than you think! Perhaps you need help from experts outside to go far down inside and settle more serious problems than rules such as these could ever cure.

7. *When we have come to terms we will put it away until we* both *agree it needs more discussing.*

A healthy union requires that you never forget some things and never remember others. Wedlock must have its lock boxes. In some of these you put certain items and throw the key away. Others you keep for later opening.

Did you notice that "both" in this rule also? If one "eyeball" glowers unduly at the "wait-a-whiles" you will do well to talk it over and maybe take out the problem for review.

One of the most infinite understandings in any husband-wife relationship is that *you can still love each other even if there are things you don't exactly like around here!*

We recently heard a luncheon speaker make the statement that no married couple should ever go to bed without talking out *everything* between them. He based his claim on the words of Paul, "Let not the sun go down on your wrath!"

We had no opportunity to talk to the man after his address but I wonder if he really meant *everything!* Paul's words sound ideal but the trouble is that, without interpretation, they are only headed in the general direction of truth.

Some scholars argue that Paul had been married. Others insist he had not. But whether he had or hadn't, if you will study all his letters you will come to the conclusion that he knew what he was about!

It was this same Paul who taught us that people filled with the right spirit will be marked by the fruits of "love, joy, peace, long-suffering, gentleness, goodness, faith, meekness, temperance!" Who could talk their way through to all of these before one day's sun goes over the hill?

So keep at it. Keep working. Keep resting. Keep trusting. Keep firing. Keep surrendering. Keep these things for later. Keep those locked forever. Keep talking. Keep listening. Keep going.

You won't reach the loftiest ranges by nightfall! But you won't need to!

If you keep giving this day all the love your hearts can produce, then tomorrow will keep giving you a larger and greater love.

For lovers who keep on keeping on with their love there is never an end to the glories of marriage.

Keep up the fight right,
Dad

"I'M SORRY, HONEY"

My dear Karen,

      The three most important words in marriage, next to "I love you" may be the humble little admission, "I'm sorry, honey!"

We have already dealt with the fact that living together in perfect harmony is more ideal than real. Even toward the one we love most there may be flashes of hatred. You will take a sensible attitude toward this. Perhaps those angry words needed to "surface." Maybe they cleared subterranean chambers to make room for more love.

Since apology is a prime ingredient in marriage, we'll give this letter to three thoughts I hope will be helpful.

1. *Some people find it difficult to express regret.*

One wife, married to a holier-than-thou husband, gave

this sad witness in our consultation together: "David is *always* on the Lord's side, and it is so hard to get along with a man who is *always* on the Lord's side!"

These are tough men to live with. It is also rough for husbands whose wives comport themselves as self-ordained saints. You will sense immediately that here is another place where the problem could have long roots. Perhaps he was taught that remorse of any kind is one form of weakness. Maybe he offered an apology once and it was rejected. Possibly you can help him ferret out the reason and set him free of one more bothersome hanger-on from his childhood.

You will do well to examine your quarreling for signs that *you* might be the guilty party this time. If you are over-defending yourself to yourself; if you are continually whipping the villain around the block with your thoughts; or feeling sorry for yourself; or mountain climbing over molehills; or sounding like a commanding officer whenever you talk; or indulging in any one of your favorite rationalizations, then this may be your day for confession. An Old Testament prophet gives us a word for those times when we "status quo" our defenses and refuse to budge: "In vain dost thou use many medicines; there is no healing for thee!"

We have been over this rocky road before in our letters, so let's move along now with this chant of the great women: *"Bigness may never begin unless it begins with me!"*

Even if it is *all* his fault, which isn't likely, you can patch up a quarrel and still keep your self-respect! If he refuses to be honest, you can be honest enough to say, "I'm sorry

72

we quarreled. Forgive me for anything I said which I shouldn't have said. There are so many things I like about you. I appreciate your love more than anything in the world, and it makes me feel just awful when we are out of sorts with each other."

Without being a phony you can make every effort to square the thing from your side. Then if he still persists, you have at least prepared your soul to receive him heartily when he is ready. It is a sick man who forever rejects the sincere "I'm waiting to love you" message from an honest woman's heart.

Apology usually requires that the most mature member of your duo makes the first move. Some marital experts say that the secret to success in the home is to change the customary fifty-fifty sharing of everything to sixty-forty. They tell us that when both members of the union are willing to go more than halfway, this couple has it made. Their wisdom applies particularly to expressing regret. We'll hope you both can develop the stretch to go more than halfway.

2. *Regrets and humor go well together.*

Some anonymous sage suggests that we take a long step forward when we can conjugate this verb:

> I am a joke
> Thou art a joke
> He is a joke
> We are jokes
> Ye are jokes
> They are jokes

It helps put our soul in order when we start the conjugation with "*I* am a joke!"

Now comes across the hills of yesterday another fact to remember. Your grandmother was fond of saying, "Don't you ever forget there are two kinds of funny. There is 'funny ha-ha' and 'funny peculiar' and you better know which is which."

This fits many places, and one of these is in the close interchange of marital expression. Excessive laughter may indicate more hysteria than good health! Some stages of marriage are no place for comedy.

Smiles are of many kinds too. You will be alert to which one of your many faces is exactly right when. Never fake the act if the play calls for a solid touch of the real thing!

But whenever a couple learns how to laugh and smile and make merry over their mistakes, a wonderful thing happens in their home. High heaven has special clean-up squads which respond to these signals. They come to sweep away the broken pieces and give that marriage a fresh beginning.

3. *Apology is one of those places in marriage where "Who did it?" or "Why did he?" or "How could she?" isn't as important as "What is the quickest way of making things right again?"*

Mr. Reed taught me a great thing. The little town where I grew up was an ideal spot for boys who loved water. One day the river authority announced a canoe race. The contest was upstream in a section which none of our gang knew. We had plenty of time to prepare, so naturally we

74

examined the course with care and practiced many hours. Mr. Reed lived along the banks where we played regularly, and he was our friend. In one of our evening visits I was complaining about the jagged stones and boulders up there. He listened to my sad story for a time. Then he stopped me with these words of wisdom, "Son," he advised, "you'll never win by fussing about the rocks. Quit worrying about them and *learn where the channels are!*"

That is a fair word for lovers. Let's say he *did* start it. Or maybe *you* are the guilty party. Possibly neither one can remember its origin. But *where* it began isn't the major matter. What counts most is *when* is it settled? With some things of love "the sooner, the better," and that rule writes itself here with a heavy hand!

Tennyson in *Idylls of the King* puts it well:

> It is the little rift within the lute
> That by and by may make the music mute!

So, if this is one of those days, go right this minute to the phone and dial his number. In your tenderest voice let the love in your heart pour itself out. Joy breaks through in an outburst of new glory, and you achieve real dignity when you discharge the obligation of your errors with these three next most important words in marriage: *"I'm sorry, honey!"*

With proper apologies,

Dad

P. S. I thought you might be interested to hear that we are working on David, the chap who is "always on the Lord's side!" I think we're making some progress. He is beginning to rearrange his pomposity. If he continues his improvement, one day I will be able to remind him that it was Moses, not David, who brought down the laws of God from Mt. Sinai!

THE "H" TWINS—
HUMILITY AND HONESTY

My dear Karen,

My favorite "Timid Soul" cartoon shows Casper Milquetoast standing on the corner in a driving rain. Water is running from the brim of his hat and, although he shivers in misery, he has finally mustered his courage to say, "If that fellow doesn't come in another forty-five minutes, *he can just go and borrow the money from somebody else!*"

Humility is often pictured like this. But to be truly humble, in the finest sense, has nothing to do with cringing before others and groveling our way through life.

One of my Quaker friends uses a term which closes in on its true meaning. When he has been "put down" by life or people or circumstances, he says with a smile, "My soul has been 'meeked!'"

77

I have heard lengthy discussions, read numerous sermons, and studied the writings of the scholars as they expound on what is meant by the phrase, "Blessed are the meek!" Their interpretations vary from something like poor Casper to potent phrases which ring with power.

Tracing it back to its original usage, I get the feeling that *to be meek means to face up to the difference between what we are and what we ought to be.*

The greatest people I know are rich with this kind of humility. The same goes for the finest marriages. You will add much to your life with each other if you can say, "Blessed are the couples who are humble and honest, for they will reach a higher love!"

Several fine things happen when you live by this beatitude. Courage to analyze yourselves, grace to apologize sincerely, patience to hold your tongues when you should, the ability to lead each other down the hall to the mirror —these are but a few of the good things which "the 'H' twins" bring along if you invite them into your home.

Let's take a look at two ugly items which will be discouraged from knocking so often at your doors if your souls are being "meeked" together.

"Gossip" is one of these. There is a familiar adage which goes, "Small minds discuss people; average minds discuss happenings; great minds discuss ideas!"

Naturally, there will be times when your talk centers on folks and days when it shares events. But you do well to check your conversation often to be sure it isn't blowing bits of outside dust and dirt into the center of your thoughts.

Judgment and "jury duty" have their place. So do censorship and criticism. But their major place is not in your home.

Whether men are as guilty as women here is open to debate. Many of us men *will* have some accounting to do at this point.

But you can develop some clever preventives if you dedicate your tongues to constructive rather than destructive talk.

A card club of my acquaintance did an interesting thing. The lady who reported this to me said, "Not one of our girls would steal money. We wouldn't steal things either. Yet we had fallen into the habit of carelessly stealing somebody's good name without thinking."

Then one brave soul dared to speak up. Since these really were women of character, they got the message and faced facts. As a corrective measure they framed this delightful wisecrack and put it in a prominent place where everyone would see it during their play:

> "I WOULDN'T SAY ANYTHING ABOUT
> HER UNLESS I COULD SAY SOMETHING
> GOOD—AND, BOY, IS THIS GOOD!"

According to them it works wonders and there is a refreshing new spirit in their fellowship. If all occupants of every home would go and do likewise, this might be an air-purifier well worth its price!

Humility and honesty may be difficult to achieve partially because it is easier to nose about in somebody else's basement than to clean up your own soot and ashes.

If you persist you won't mature to the greatness in you. When you go down "their" stairs you yourselves go down. If you turn your steps upward to their better points you go up. Here is one of those universal laws which works no other way.

To allow yourselves this "we-are-good-but-they-are-not-so-good" attitude will eventually dirty up your bridge of communication and make it unattractive to both.

"Nagging" is among the major gripes heard in my study. For some reason, more husbands bring me this complaint than women. Again, I'm not certain that wives do it more than their men, but I'm sure of this—one way to keep him loving you is to avoid carping and harping of any kind.

Those who overdo here may need to travel back down the paths of their personal histories to discover some reasons for their censorious natures. Perfectionism is one of the most common sources. Whenever a child is brought up by adults whose spirit is "nothing but the best from you will satisfy us," that child may develop a pointed tongue. A severe upbringing which ingrains unnatural standards is almost certain to create dissatisfaction with everything and everybody.

Men who must live with women of this temperament do not become more teachable. They only build up their defenses that much higher and finally erect soundproof barriers in their ears. Or, if their hearing apparatus is not equipped to do this, they stay away from the juggernaut of charges and countercharges which their marriage has become. Working overtime when they don't need to, excessive drinking, philandering, and, finally, their lawyer's office may be havens of rest compared to the wild winds of their woman's words!

One such man described his wife with this damning statement: "She'd make an excellent district attorney! She has her process-servers out for my faults, and she keeps them working seven days a week, twenty-four hours a day!

That's a pitiful statement, isn't it! I regret that there are others to match it in every hamlet and city. So, when you find yourself even slightly inclined in this direction, stop right there and turn the process-servers inside you.

"The 'H' twins" will bring their own cleaning equipment if you give them access to every nook and cranny. But these fact-finding crews have an uncomfortable way of always starting with "number one" or they refuse to start. Eventually, they may move their buckets and mops to the other side of the union but don't ask them to commence there. They never do!

"*My* soul has been meeked!" is how my Quaker friend puts it. I trust you'll have the wisdom and grace to join those feminine lovelies who know that he has his words in their right order.

If you had the wings of an angel you'd probably be ready for heaven and, though we all hope to make it eventually, we're more likely to arrive there when we say, and mean it, "My soul, *thou* ailest here and here!"

From one side of your family you come out of stock which found it terribly hard to open the inner box and face the devils there. But from the other side you have learned that there is no other road to inner peace.

This is tough stuff we're dealing with here. May you have the largeness of soul to *examine yourself first* in humility and honesty.

Yours for true meekness together,
Dad

P. S. I just remembered this one woman who said: "I was operating under the delusion that I needed a new husband. Then one day it occurred to me that perhaps my husband needed a new wife!"

GETTING THROUGH
TO THE REAL SELF

My dear Karen,

It is very important for you to understand this about men. Most of their day is spent in an impersonal world.

In certain professions what the man *does* matters more than how he really *feels*. In some jobs what he *produces* for his company is more important in their eyes than *how he thinks*.

Modern business is so developed that the person is often eclipsed behind the almighty dollar, and a man's real self may be seriously repressed.

Because of this, a man will do almost anything for a woman who can get through to the inner man.

Here is an example of what I mean. You will not remember this because you were little.

This leader in the church, father of two grown daughters, gave up his wife and married the elevator girl.

I wasn't the only one horrified. The whole town was undone when he sold his successful business and moved to another state to start over. It seemed for a time in our community that there was nothing else going on in the world except this.

But I want to pass on some lines he shared with me when he came to say goodbye. We had been the best of friends, and we could talk heart-to-heart. When it came the moment for some word of explanation, this is the way he put it:

"Charlie, I don't expect you to understand, but let me tell you how it started. One day we were alone in the elevator going up. Just before she opened the door at my floor she laid her hand on my arm and said, 'Please don't think me forward, but I want you to know I think you are the kindest man in this whole building. For four years I've watched you tip your hat to the ladies and smile. Only you do it differently from other men. With you it's more as if it came from your heart. I just wanted to say thank you for being what you are.' "

Then he went on to explain that over the weeks they began to visit and he discovered what she meant. She had been married twice before and she told him, "Both these men *treated me as if I were a thing.*" That, he said, was the statement which lit the fires because that's how he felt about himself. He had been a faithful husband, and I knew it. He had been a good father, and I knew this also. That he had been a fine provider the whole town could see.

But there was one thing lacking and this is how he described it: "My wife didn't love me *for me!* She loved me *for herself!* She 'used' me so my daughters did it, too. I didn't realize until I met another empty heart such as mine *how much it means to be loved because you are you!"*

That's what the man said. He gave up status, investments, leadership, a secure future. He turned his back on all this for an elevator girl who got through to share the real self with him.

I never could discuss it with the forsaken wife. We had been friends, too, but she pulled down the shades on her heart now and refused to talk about it. He said no more than these few lines I've shared with you.

But I can pass on a few things I've picked up through the years since that first shocking experience. I've seen it happen many times, and there are certain things which *will not* be conducive to your man's opening his full self to you. In our fourth letter we discussed the freedom factor which will work toward his unfolding. We've considered honesty and apology as additional helps toward self-disclosure. We'll see to others later. But right now, I'd suggest you eliminate three words from your marriage and keep them erased if you hope to get through all the way.

1. *"Ridicule!"*

Of course, he'll have some wild ideas. Every thinker does. But when he comes up with one, hear him out in rapt attention. This may represent something which came to him in a flash at the office. He's been asking himself, "Have I made a brilliant discovery, or are there 'bugs' here which I don't see?" He'd like to be sure before he presents it to his superiors. He knows that men often judge men by their ability to consider every angle before they go off half-cocked.

Let's say it again! Most of us husbands are required to live behind some partial facade in our positions. We see things which we know are true. We see others we know are wrong. Yet "politics" or "timing" or "expediency" may call for sublimation. We also sense that though we check things dozens of times in the secret of our minds we may miss some errors which show up when our thoughts are expressed aloud. All this makes home that much more attractive if we can share our repressed thoughts knowing that they will get a full hearing with no hint of derision.

So, let him talk even if he is far out in left field and you know it. Don't cut him off too soon. Perhaps he'll discover the flaw for himself in free expression. A mature man gets a real thrill from catching on to his own loose thinking. But if he doesn't see and you do, pace yourself now! There will be plenty of time later for you to bring him carefully back where the facts are.

You can laugh *with* him. You can tell him he's the funniest in fun. But never laugh *at* the things he shares with you until he laughs first. Ridicule in small doses or large will clam any man eventually.

2. *"Overfastidiousness!"*

This is a long word and it would take too much time to spell it out in all its meanings. The reason is that some men like one type of neatness and some another. But my observation is that the perfectionist wife is generally heading for trouble.

This applies both to keeping the house and keeping yourself.

No home is likely to represent the acme of loveliness for a man unless there is something here which seems to say, "Come! Let down, way down!" If the whole place is so impeccably kept that it smacks of stiffness, you may discourage his self-disclosure.

Same goes for you. The "china-doll-mustn't-touch" look is for china dolls. It is true that women are to admire and behold in their loveliness. You'll want him to be proud of your clothes and the way you wear them. Cleanliness of garment and person is also of prime importance, as any girl knows who has eyes for the ads or ears for commercials. So, both in public and for him alone, you'll keep yourself with these things in mind. But the well-groomed woman wears something else with her fresh garments and her cologne. It is that subtle invitation which seems to say, "Come touch me! Take me in your arms!"

This is an art to be learned. It varies with each wife because each husband has his own peculiar likes and dislikes. But it is a wise woman who knows that every man is equipped, both body and soul, with a subconscious radar which seeks some place to let himself go.

3. *"Pushiness!"*

Most husbands also have something inside which automatically erects barriers against the wife who is forever pointing out how much better his friends are doing in the economic world. So, Joe did get to be vice-president!

Maybe Vincent doesn't want to do it the way Joe did it! Maybe he doesn't want it—period! Praise him for his accomplishments, but don't wave continually before him the honors of others.

There is a secret gnawing in the heart of any man who feels that he is constantly measured not on his own merits but against the merits of others. Excessive pushing from a woman is one sure "detacher" in marriage. Few males will let down freely in the presence of the "drive-drive-drive" female!

The same thing goes if you shove him around socially until he is out of character. If, during the day, he feels that he must live with a mask for prudence' sake, then he will all the more appreciate friends who feel "natural" and allow him to feel the same.

Evenings and weekends and "free" hours have a special meaning to most men. Of course, they are precious for women, too. Whether being a housewife calls for as much role-playing as that of the breadwinner may be open to discussion. But there is no debating the fact that the man who must live most of his working time in partial cover-up will be grateful for a wife who understands his predicament and provides him a place to be his true self.

One of the challenges we face often in life is to discover the fine line between enough and too much. This is true in these three things.

You must work for an atmosphere where you can tell the whole truth. But this generally comes only after you have proven yourself a sounding-board which never gives off one hint of ridicule.

You will make every effort to keep your house and yourself tidy and clean. But you won't overdo it.

You are wise to let him have a big say in what you belong to, who you go with, and what he can do without your hammering comparison to the accomplishments of others.

This creation of true person-to-person transparency is another of the big things which marriage is about.

It will not come easily! Breaking up the protective crusts we have built around us may be slow business. Sometimes it is painful. Because this is true, there will be times of inner resistance from each side. But don't let these continue too long. It is good to constantly measure your progress and make certain that your opening to each other is moving in the direction of increasing revelation.

You better believe it, my darling daughter—a man will do almost anything for a woman with whom he can learn to share his real self.

With high hopes for getting through,

Dad

THE BABY AND
THE MUSCLE MAN

My dear Karen,

The concept of "Papa, the strong protector" and "Mama, the clinging vine" is a favorite theme for melodrama. But in real life it's like the song with the murderous grammar—" 'Taint necessarily so!"

You will be wise to remember that your husband has a little boy in his makeup somewhere. This may be one of those things you can't trace back to its origin. Or maybe you can.

One day I had a frantic call from a desperate father. He pompously announced that I must see his son at once. Things had been going from bad to worse. They needed help "right this very minute, by gad!" Junior was "raising hell at home, raising hell at school, raising hell all over the place." (I'm quoting this father, see?)

So we cleared the calendar, and Junior turned out to be one of the biggest fourteen-year-olds ever to plunk himself down in any pastor's study.

The father introduced us. No response! Next, he admonished his young one with great vigor, "Tell the man what's troubling you, son!" No response.

This pop-to-pop monologue continued for another try, and another, and another, and—then the light! It flashed long enough for me to see this: I would never know whether this monster was deaf and dumb unless we could unload father.

So in my sternest voice I said, "Will you step into the library for a few minutes, please? I'd like to speak with your son in private."

At last we were alone.

It would be more in the interest of accurate reporting if I said *I* was alone!

Though Junior was free to open his mouth and release all his pent-up emotion to "the man," he said not a word.

Quite by accident I began fingering the gold football on my watch chain. I often do this when I'm contemplating the right move.

Then suddenly the dam gates opened. I never did understand all he said that time. But after considerable babbling he came through distinctly minus the gibberish.

"I hate footballs. I'm never going to like footballs, and *will you please stop playing with that awful football?*"

To cut across a long series of visits and many months, let's turn to the last chapter for a peek at the "whodunit" pages.

You guessed it! The real villain was that pushy, pushy pop.

When we finally made a breakthrough on the adult side of the problem, dad confessed that he had been a frustrated football player in his own high school days. (You must not blame the coaches. For good teamwork, everyone *has* to shut up in the huddle to hear the signals.)

So he was inwardly ashamed of his failure. He played it like an old record—"I've been trying to make an athlete out of him since he was three. That's how lots of the stars got their start, you know. But all he does is sit around the house and eat. Never does anything constructive. Besides, he needs the exercise. You agree, don't you, that athletics are good for young boys? I had a talk with the coach and he said this son of mine would be a cinch for all-conference if he cared even a little. He could go to State and get him a scholarship. Then they pay big bonuses in the pros, you know. You've got to remember things like that—" and so on *ad nauseam*.

Right there father put his big mouth to the real trouble, didn't he? Junior did *not* care "even a little." He had never cared "even a little."

But the story has one happy phase to its ending. Junior did care about one thing, and you'll be surprised when I tell you that he's playing a big part this Friday night. It's not on the football team. He is one of the school's star actors in the senior play. *That's* what he wanted—drama!

What became of the villain? I am pleased to report that two or three psychiatrists, numerous doctor bills, and a few years later father seems to have caught on to one fact. It costs to keep your mouth in high gear all the time.

He isn't completely cured, and the doctor warns that perhaps he never will be. But at least he's changed his tune to something Junior can live with. Today, pop is proclaiming in the streets that "the Hollywood scouts are rumored to be on hand this very Friday. And, by gad, do you know why they're coming? It's to see my Junior, that's why. They pay big money for actors, you know." . . . et cetera, et cetera.

I have been glad to see father and son sitting side by side in church these last few weeks. His current psychotherapist *is* a dandy! For years this sad dad could not attend divine service with his family. He could sing, and read the litanies, and such as that. But even a poor sermon takes at least twenty minutes and—oh, shucks! You get the point!

Junior wanted to grow up *his* way, and his dad wouldn't let him. This fourteen-year-old giant wasn't really raising all that hell. But you know who was!

There are many ways to raise people, several ways to raise arguments, and one sure way to raise hell. This is to pressure someone near you into doing it your way, by gad, or else!

So there will be times when Vincent will wish to go back to his childhood and live it over again. He'll want to play like he is a little boy.

This is mostly subconscious. Perhaps he doesn't even realize that some part of him was forced out of infancy too soon. (I'm doing some psychological reading by a famous authority who holds that every person on earth struggles sometimes to get back into the womb where life was warm and free from care.)

Some of this is over my head but the part I can understand makes sense. I'm sure it will also have meaning for
you. I hope it will because you must allow your husband
now and then to put his head in your lap and be thoroughly mothered.

Now, let's talk about muscles. I've never had sufficient
time with the head doctor who works on Junior's dad to
ask if his wife knew anything about the male ego and
how to assuage it.

It wouldn't be fair to blame her anyway. She may have
given her very best and not even reached first base. But
you will if you teach yourself that sometimes your little
boy wishes to step stage-forward as the big, brave man. At
these moments he wants you to be "oohing" and "aahing"
as you behold all that hair on his chest. He prefers that
you swoon a bit in tribute to his biceps and triceps.

Whenever you sense him getting ready for this act, run
quick for the soapbox and place it firmly under his feet.
Sit there before him with stars in your pretty eyes. Give
him the "what-would-I-ever-do-without-you-to-protect-me"
treatment. Praise God every time this happens and en-
courage him to exercise the Tarzan calling to his mate
from within.

When we started we stated that this kind of stuff makes
excellent script for melodrama. But a little of it also goes
well in the real-life drama of love between a wise wife and
the lucky man who has one.

Chekhov warned that his plays would be exasperating to
the public unless they clearly understood his purpose. His
responsibility as a playwright, he said, was only to state

94

the problem. It was up to his audiences to work out their own solutions.

It is unfortunate perhaps that we come to some points in these letters where I must bid adieu like Chekhov.

This is one of those places. I can tell you how it is with men. I can tell you that you must learn these secrets. But, not being a woman, that's all I can tell you.

Since we have now reached a dead end, let's close this particular letter with a beatitude. We'll call this, "Beatitude of a Fortunate Male."

Blessed is the man with a wife who admires her husband for the might of his manhood, but coddles him now and then as a mother comforteth her child.

Yours for some "oohs" and "aahs"
plus the maternal instinct,

Dad

SEX IS A SACRAMENT

My dear Karen,

On that first night when he signs "Mr. and Mrs." to the hotel register, you are entering a physical relationship which we hope will be "out of this world" in more ways than one.

Sex is a sacrament. What goes on between you bodily that night and through the years to come is one of God's precious gifts to his own.

I hope you will come to understand that this part of life is not a duet. It is a trinity. You are really having a relationship with a wise Creator who made your bodies different for his purposes.

So, begin your sex life together on the premise that this is God's love you are sharing here. This is beautiful. This is holy. This is sacred.

When it reaches its best between you, it bursts in heavenly raptures you never knew were hidden within.

It will probably take some doing from both parties to get things started on such a platform. For one thing, society hasn't helped you. You have seen cheap sex in the movies and read it in books. You have heard it vulgarized in off-color stories. You have reviewed its brutal headlines in the papers. It has been displayed before you in advertisements for deodorants and dance halls, macaroni and mascara, soft drinks, shaving lotion, tires, trucks, cigars, cigarettes, and cigarillos.

Now, suddenly, you are expected to lift all this subliminal exposure up to the high level where it belongs? The answer is, of course, same song, next verse—it will take time and it will take effort on your part.

This will not happen all at once, and this is where so many couples make their first serious mistake. They assumed that marriage would automatically bring them where the blessed are. This is simply not so, and you'll be prepared best if you understand that building a heavenly sex life is one of the goals toward which your mating moves. Sometimes its pace is slower than you would like. Occasionally it takes a nice leap forward. Now and then it reaches a plateau. Then it gets moving once more. But, whatever the cadence, it does take time.

Another reason why you might have difficulty touching the stars immediately could be traced to whatever guilt-conscience you bring into your union. This may be some old slip which you thought you had safely buried. These ghosts have a way of pushing over tombstones at the most inappropriate time and leering, "Remember me?"

Or it might be that your courting habits have produced an anxiety you'll find hanging on when it should go away. During your engagement period, you may even have fallen into the practice of quarreling as a release from sexual tension. I have known some married couples who kept right on fussing out of habit when they no longer needed this outlet. You will be alert to all this and remember that it may take a while for official news of the wedding to get all the way through to your inner tribunal. You can help each other with these things. In gentleness and understanding, by patience and tenderness, you make your bed and lie in it for better things in the days to come.

There might even be other reasons why sex is somewhat less than sensational all at once. Sometimes there are unfortunate childhood memories to be overcome. Perhaps certain false impressions were picked up at an early age and have never been clarified. But most of your neurotic repressions will give way gradually provided that you (a) are honest with each other and (b) "love one another with a pure heart fervently."

(You are well aware that there are sources of professional help for those who reach an impasse after giving it their all. But don't bother your pretty head about this sort of thing right now. I've come to appreciate Vincent for many reasons and one of these is his innate soft touch where it matters. It matters right here, so be grateful for sex and let yourself go.)

Let's go back now to where we started. Sex is a sacrament. It is communion of the highest kind. For you, it is communion between Vincent and Karen. It is communion with life at its virile best. But, above all, it is communion with the Lord who created human bodies for other purposes than reproduction of the species alone.

Sex is tapping the deep-flowing rhythms of the universe. It is uniting with the same power which turns the earth in its orbit, pumps sap to the top of the tree, sets out the stars at night, moves water down the river, brings two hearts to stand one day and read life's meaning in each other's eyes. In this phase of marriage, you are actually tuning-in to the creative processes which are far greater than ever man might have done on his own.

In the first chapter of our Bibles there is the beautiful story of our creation. It was obviously written by some ancient wise man to give us the good news that we are not mere accidents going somewhere to happen.

Before this initial chapter of life's most sacred writing has ended, it tells us that in his perfectly marvelous way of doing things the Creator included this wonder of wonders—"male and female created he them." If you will read that chapter again you will note this majestic observation in the closing verse: *"And God saw everything that he had made, and behold, it was very good."*

Your mother and I can witness firsthand to the truth of this all-inclusive statement. I have counseled with many other husband-wife combinations who would heartily join this song of praise to the Lord who reviewed with pleasure all that he had done.

And among the best of his good
things is sex at its best,

Dad

SEXUAL DIFFERENCES, MALE AND FEMALE

My dear Karen,

They say that no two people in the world are alike. Most of us do have two eyes, one nose, a specified number of teeth, five fingers on each hand, and certain other things in common. Yet the statement is true if you take into account all that goes into the making of each individual life.

This will become increasingly obvious as you ponder the truth that no two people have been raised in the same way. Environments differ so much that inevitable variances are part of the background in even the most compatible marriages.

Likewise, heredity factors have shaped him in one pattern and fashioned her from quite a different mold.

Then, in addition to all this, there is another important

point for your agenda. There are some distinct differences between men and women just because that's how they were created in the first place.

For example, man is likely to be objective and abstract. Woman is generally subjective and concrete. Man's world of creativity and occupational involvement tends to center his attention outside the home. Woman's most important goings-on will probably focus more on the family.

Because this is true, it is easier for most men to interpret their world in an impersonal manner. Some of us have learned the hard way that women often take things more personally than men.

They forgot to teach us this in school, and it was their mistake. Those of us who work closely with both genders soon find out that you can level with most men and they level back, and then you go drink coffee together as the best of friends. But working with women requires an altogether different set of gears. Many a neophyte (I speak from experience) has stripped some very important cogs in the machinery before he caught on to the difference.

Happy marriage depends in part on making allowances for these essential variances. You can even learn to appreciate such things and let them complement each other in your union.

This will also save you many tears when he doesn't immediately share your enthusiasm for the new drapes or become as overjoyed as you are about baby's first tooth. You also do well to remember these innate divergencies when he brings home some worry from the office and sits with that far-away look in his eye. You might be taking personally something which isn't even remotely related to what you are thinking. What you interpret as a slight on his part may be only a reflection of his being a man and your being a woman.

Now, let's relate this to your sex life.

For many couples, sex begins with general disappointment, moves on to become recurrently disruptive, and at last is quite insipid. Some of these muddled marriages got that way because husband and wife never faced up to this truth—there are some natural biological differences between male and female.

What are they?

Let's examine a couple of real importance.

1. *Sex probably has deeper meanings to the woman than it does to her man.*

On first thought this may surprise you.

Many a wife in consultation has said things such as this: "It seems that all my husband ever thinks about is sex. He interprets every move I make as a mating move. Do *all* men figure *all* of life by sex symbols *all* the time?"

When you examine this sort of thing carefully you observe an important fact. Man's seeming obsession with sex does not prove that it means more to the male than female. On the contrary, it may mean the opposite. His sex drive is more of a surface, physical thing. Yours is likely to be much deeper, a matter of spirit and soul. He is more easily aroused. Your stirrings come from farther away inside yourself.

One sweet little wife said something to me I'd like to share with you. She, too, had been awed at the apparently insatiable sex appetite of her husband. Unfortunately it was also obvious that he was a clumsy clod in his approaches.

So we discussed this difference-in-the-sexes theme and then she said wistfully: "I had always thought that sex begins at breakfast. A few tender words to start things off would mean so much. Then perhaps a phone call sometime during the day. Some endearments exchanged when he comes home and maybe some help with the supper dishes. Talking things over after the children are in bed. Exchanging ideas. Discussing what we've been doing during the day. A love pat here and a few kisses at the right time. I guess I've had the wrong idea. I thought maybe sex could begin at breakfast, build up during the day, and then explode in bed at night!"

The facts are that she is one hundred percent correct in her analysis of how it ought to be. She couldn't have said it better. That's what it should be like for most women! And it is a wise man who learns this skill and seeks to become an artist at playing on his wife's heartstrings.

I wish for you such a virtuoso. These men are rare and, there's that drum again—they don't often come ready-built this way.

Which leads to the second biological difference you must recognize:

2. *Most men need sex more often than women.*

No rules can be laid down which apply to every marriage. Frequency of intercourse is something each couple must work out for themselves. Some couples in union may be happy with gratification once each week. Others would find this much too little sexual fare for their more vigorous appetites. There are certain marriages where sex is a beautiful part of every day's experience. Because each human being is different, it follows that each combination of human beings will vary. It is also likely that even the most thoroughly mated couples will differ from time to time and perhaps season to season. For this reason, to apply the same standards for every marriage would be sheer folly.

You do well to remember always that quality is more important than quantity in nearly everything you can mention. But from the marriages I have seen in consultation, it is apparent that *how often* usually matters most to the man and the *how to* is most important to the woman.

Yet, no matter the frequency, the main thing is to come to it joyfully. Learn to rest with it. The majority of wives who complain that it exhausts them will find their weariness in their head. Of course, there are variations in every rule and sometimes physical problems should be examined. There are even exceptions to the fact that most men like to think of themselves as sexual athletes. Some women complain that their husbands are never interested. This is not how it should be, and it needs looking into by the experts when it becomes a problem.

There may also be days when even the most vigorous man is so sapped of energy by his real or imaginary troubles that he is devoid of sexual desire. Don't become hysterical and don't take it personally if this happens now and then. You will learn to read him well and be wise enough to graciously decline sometimes for his sake. Perhaps he's done to exhaustion now and you'd do well to quiet your own interest. In marriage, it is best to measure emotions against the bigger background of time and effort and tender, loving care.

However, there will be no exception to this rule: You are a prudent wife when you look on sex, in part, as your opportunity to be a blessing to your husband. The tender women train themselves to receive a large measure of contentment just from contenting their men.

It is not true, in my counseling experience, that both parties to the union *need* the same results every time. I have read some writers who say that a man must be able to bring his wife to climax on every occasion of sexual love. In my judgment there is just one thing wrong with this supposition—it simply isn't so.

Some women tell me that they love to minister to their husband's emotional needs even when they care nothing at all about physical culmination for themselves.

I suspect that there are many marriages which could be considerably improved if both parties properly understood and accepted this. Some men have been falsely informed that they are failures if they cannot put their wives into ecstasy every time they reach that point themselves. This may be nothing short of selfishness on the man's part. He does wrong to set up goals which only meet some neurotic need of his own. How often he brings her to fruition should be *her* choice, not his. It takes a wise young husband to understand that his wife needs to be treated not as the passionate creature he dreamed about in teen fantasies, or read about in cheap sex books, or heard described with lurid words by the amateur in the locker room.

She needs to be treated as the woman she is! You can help him comprehend this if you can convince him that

105

part of the time your only satisfaction-need is for him to be satisfied. In other words, you can have a mental enthusiasm for closeness even when your body is not enthusiastic in the same way as his.

But this must not continue forever. There are times when a husband is happier if his wife's exuberance matches his own. As we have said, it is usually true that man is the initial center of passion. Then sometimes she must become a center of passion on the occasions of her own choosing. At other times they become the center of passion together.

This is delicate doing and you must love it, work at it, and care enough to make it whatever is natural and good for the two of you.

A few paragraphs back we touched on a matter worth another look. You are wise to discuss together what you were taught about sex in your teens. Unfortunately, many parents even today have not presented this side of life to their children in a healthy way. Some boys picked up all they know about sex in the low places of other minds. Some girls grew up in a vacuum here. Others got their ideas by osmosis from a mother whose concept of women and sex was "this is our fate, this martyrdom!" It will help you both to know more about your own mental histories on this subject. Scared little girls and sex-obsessed boys don't come built that way in the first place. We are all partly what we picked up on the way, and this is another reason why gentleness is very much in order during the early seasons of nuptial love. It is also one more visible evidence that sex as a sacrament is the right basic concept.

There is one more thing to remember about wise wives and husbands whose sex drive seems unquenchable. The smart girls do not ration their men. They do not prescribe time, nor place, nor frequency, nor circumstances, nor manner. In my next letter I'll tell you more about these things, but right here let's run this by for a look:

I have known dozens of men who left home for sexual entertainment and many of them belonged to women who insisted on always dictating the terms!

There is one other death knell to sexual happiness which you should guard carefully. This is sounded whenever a woman thinks of sex as a prize to be awarded when he has been an especially good boy. Whenever she holds it out to him as a bribe, she contributes a number one prospect for the women who go for casual affairs.

The truth is that both "boughten sex" and "getting it on the side" are never completely satisfying. They couldn't be. If sex is holy and if it needs the compassion of true concern to make it complete, then you will see this at once —substitutes are really not preferable to most men. But many males do settle for "seconds." Sometimes it is the woman they would love to love fully who has driven them to their revolt.

It's big, big business, isn't it? I hope you're not growing weary of the theme that marriage at its best is a lifework for two people at their best.

Mature partnership is an artistic achievement which doesn't come as a lucky row of beans on a bingo card. Sex may be one of nature's instincts, but it is not "natural" in the same sense as the casual, largely self-centered, and sometimes violent manner of the lower animals.

But men are like animals in this sense—they are much more ready on quick notice than the opposite of the species. Most young men come into marriage with a large reservoir of frustration which has accumulated through their growing years. This is one reason it is important for you to keep from having babies too soon. If enough time passes before that precious third party enters the scene, Vincent will make a better husband in the long run. Not only is it essential that you learn to adjust to each other before you both must adjust to number three—it is good for you both if you can thoroughly clear your systems of the things you had to backlog before it was legal.

If a baby comes quickly, of course you will love the little darling and do your best with the circumstances at hand. But the child will have a better mother and father if they have spent plenty of time learning each other and pouring out their love to each other with no competition for the first few years.

You have always loved children, and you'll be a perfectly wonderful mother after the manner of your own. But, take it from me, your man needs sex and lots of it even when it may be the farthest thing from your mind. Convince him if you can that you love him so much you enjoy sharing your charms with him simply because he is in the mood for more.

Here is another beatitude for you. Let's call it, "Beatitude for an always-warm marriage": *Blessed is the woman who can celebrate her husband's virility with a true generosity that often seeks not so much to be loved as to love.*

Gratefully,
Dad

THE SAINT AND THE
SWEET LITTLE SINNER

My dear Karen,

Early in our marriage a wise clergyman friend of your mother's gave her what he called his "description of the ideal wife." At first reading it may seem a bit risqué. But when you turn it around in your mind a few times you'll come to see that it is more good sense than impropriety.

The perfect mate for any man, said he, is: *"An angel in the home and a devil in bed!"*

Most men have an innate hope that their wife will be a combination of that old phrase, "The saint and the sweet little sinner!"

But the wives I have known who could qualify for such accolades are in the minority. I see their opposite often in

109

consultation. Some of them proudly announce, "I never refused him!" They remind me of hopeful heroes waiting in line for the purple heart.

That might be the worst thing you could say about your marriage. Any man gets weary if he must always make the first move. Perhaps you'll join the hosts who chant, "But my man never gets weary!" Actually, however, his constant demand may be the very outgrowth of his weariness.

So, let's start with this, and I'll give you a few pointers on becoming the saintly little demon who can keep her man the kind of man she wants him to be.

1. *Be sexually aggressive some of the time.*

Do you remember when we played hide-and-seek? It was lots of fun for everyone. But to play the game right you had to take your turn as seeker now and then.

The same thing is true of sex, and there are some profound reasons behind this.

Never forget that Vincent wants to be wanted. The fact that sex is more of a surface matter to men does not eliminate the male depth-factor completely. You can count on this: Your husband longs to believe that he's wonderful enough for you to yearn sometimes for his sexual companionship.

It matters everything to a man if he has a home where he knows he is of inestimable value as a man. The world may deflate him, but he will be restored within his own walls. He may be wounded deeply out there in the marketplace, but at home there is a balm for him. Your husband can stand much more in the rough and tumble of a cutthroat world if you have convinced him that there is a waiting emotional center where he is vitally important.

You will study his ups and downs and learn to read well his soul's condition. The more he feels frustrated in his plans; the day he has been roughly handled by his superiors; when the big contract did not come through, or if in any way you sense that he has been put down somewhere —this is the time when you move in to indicate that your whole soul and body would welcome a closeness to him. Sex is a God-ordained means of assuring your partner that he is the most important person in the world right here, right now.

Actually, no matter how well things are going there is a measure of basic loneliness in every heart, male or female. I suspect that much of the moral laxity of our day is not alone immorality for immorality's sake. Some of it is a crying of the human soul for belonging. By sex, when it is right, we move out of our island existence to become a part of the mainland.

Glands are in need of release and sex is a biological clearance worth everything to the man who needs this cleansing. But it is much more than that. It is a confidence booster, a solace for injured pride, a psychological upward thrust when his soul cries out for a lift.

The surprise element is also a welcome feature to most men. Some night on your way home from somewhere, one day on a picnic just for the two of you, on the beach, in the woods, anywhere under the sun or the moon and stars where you are safe together—these are moments men cherish forever. This is a truth to build on. He will love you more with his soul if you overwhelm him now and then when he wasn't expecting your need for his body.

Learn to interpret him well and you be the seeker some of the time. Because most men think about sex more than women, the proper amount of aggression in you will add zest to his anticipation.

2. *Don't be afraid of experiment and variety.*

There is no need for me to write you a manual on sexual procedures. You have attended courses in marriage, and there are excellent books on this theme for those who need them.

The main thing I want to say here is that sex ought to be fun. It is not meant to be deadly serious all the time.

If you are to discover its fullest joys, you must come to this relationship as uninhibited as you can possibly be. You should give each other freedom to love in whatever way comes naturally to you both.

Some wives have never been told that the unusual may occur, and, when it does, this should be examined by both partners to the union as naturally as possible. Many women simply lack the knowledge that there are numerous positions and interesting variations.

So this is worth remembering: *There is nothing wrong with anything you may wish to do in your sex life provided it is pleasing to you both and not harmful to either.*

My heart goes out to the horror-stricken who come for counseling because of some "awful" suggestion their husband suddenly presented. They tell their story haltingly, and the word "perverted" is often included in their account. Perhaps somewhere in your girlhood you picked up ideas of perversion which have stayed with you. This term ordinarily makes reference to relations between members of one sex. When it refers to marriage, it means that one member of the union forces the other resulting in his or her psychological hurt.

You must teach yourself that nothing is perverted nor ugly nor unclean between you and Vincent if it is a new intimacy shared out of mutual desire for something novel and a fuller yearning for each other.

Some couples will be wise enough to know that certain unusual developments may be born out of neurotic needs which have never been satisfied. We have discussed the fact that many men carry with them into adulthood the infant's longing to be thoroughly related to the mother.

It is my experience in counseling that men who had a "weak" mother-son connection may be particularly fascinated by experimental sex. If hers was a "smother-love" or some other attempt to dominate; if he still clings emotionally to her in an unnatural way; or if he felt a maternal neglect and never really touched "home base" there; then there may be all kinds of unusual ideas in him which need working through. (Once again, you must realize that there are exceptions to every rule in these deep inner entanglements.) But you can best help him understand himself by talking it out together, by tenderness in inner research, and by a sex life which is complete in every way desirable to you both.

Remember the rule: Whatever increases the pleasure of sexual intimacy is right if it is mutually desired and if it leads to complete sexual gratification without harm.

You may be sure that you are not inventing something for the world. Everything imaginable here has been tried and tested. But if you keep an open mind and a joyful heart, you may discover some great new thrills for yourselves.

3. *Keep your body as alluring as God meant it to be.*

One afternoon at five I was calling on a church member when she suddenly stood up, turned toward the door and said, "Now, if you will excuse me, Dr. Shedd, John comes home in half an hour and I always spend the last thirty minutes before he arrives getting myself ready for him."

She did this quite naturally. Then when she realized that she had asked me to leave she blushed and was very embarrassed.

But not I! I inwardly rejoiced for women such as this. I commended her highly without reserve, and as I went down the walk I caught myself humming, "Ah, Sweet Mystery of Life!" As I drove along headed straight for home, I thought how much better our world would be if every woman spent the same thirty minutes in like manner. I should also add that this particular woman has five children of variant sizes and all of school age. Don't ask me how she has organized them for this ritual! I'm not a woman so I don't know. But I do know this, her husband is very much in love with her.

Some women grow "dutchy" the minute that ring is on their finger. They wear clothes about the house which would go better at a hard-times party. There is simply no excuse for some of the things I see on women. I have found housewives, during the day, wearing color combinations which remind me of our friend Harrison McGill's classic remark. As he viewed that perfectly awful rug some "generous" soul had donated to the choir room, he said in amazement, "There simply is no such color as that, is there?"

Vincent may say he will love you no matter how you look. He may not seem to mind if you get fat and out of shape. But then again—there was that early date when someone at the school dance didn't see him come in with you on his arm. So this inquisitive buddy tapped him on the shoulder and, pointing to you, he asked, "Who's the new babe with the cute build?" Your man will never forget that night.

You are a beautiful girl, and there isn't any reason why you can't keep him figure-proud of his wife for a long time. And if you remember the wedding vows, he promises to love you "for better, for worse, for richer, for poorer," but there is no mention of loving "through thick and thin."

Of course, it's harder after the babies come. But you're up against the stiffest competition in the marketplace these days. It's all over the place. Don't forget that these sirens do have a drawing power which is something to reckon with. From what I've seen, the best way to deal with this is to make it look pale and lusterless compared to what waits with open arms at his own address. There is no road to any other female so attractive to a healthy husband as the road home to his wife if he can share with her, either silently or openly, his inmost feelings both high and low.

If you're doing your homework, you'll not need to worry either when you are out together and he turns his head to review some passing arrangement of molecules which

115

smacks of sex appeal. You have done a good thing when you can get him to share with you what he likes and does not like in other women.

The fact that you are married to each other does not mean that you will now be blind to the attractive features of others. There may even be fleeting moments during the sex act itself when minds which love each other deeply will stray a bit. Happy is the marriage where each partner can clear thoughts which need to go.

Take care also to dress yourself in the loveliest things you can afford in preparation for your intimate moments together. I think I have told you about my fine old assistant pastor who looked on me more as a son than as his fellow worker. He never had a boy and he loved to "father" me. So he would advise me on almost everything, and this is another gem your mother and I hold dear: "Son," he said, "you've got to save money somewhere, but there are two places where you should not cut down ever. Never try to save on food nor women's lingerie!"

This is sage advice from a salty saint who had a successful fifty years of love to back up his statement. Among your husband's most precious memories when he is not in your presence are these recollections of beauty shared when you were together.

The female of our species was created with seductive powers which have been debauched by sinners and maligned by moralists through the years. But do you suppose the world simply hasn't grown up to this truth—maybe women were made that way because that's how they are needed at the right time and in the right place?

History makes it plain that every civilization which has

lost respect for marital fidelity has been relegated to the dump heap of material no longer useable for eternal construction.

The best protection I know against loose sex is a wife who knows the glories of womanhood and uses her natural charms to the maximum.

With high hopes for heavenly rapture,
Dad

THOSE GREAT BIG
BEAUTIFUL DOLLARS

My dear Karen,

In our married days at the seminary we went often to the warehouses on grocer's row. There was one place where they stacked cans of food clear up to the ceiling. It was like standing before a mountain of tin. There were big cans, little cans, tall cans, short cans, round, square, oblong, flat—cans of every size, shape, and condition.

There was, however, this one difference between the cans here and those you see on your grocer's shelves. *These had no labels.* Because of this slight omission they were for sale at three cents per can. The sorters had tossed them aside as "damaged," which meant anything from a major dent to some minor flaw which could only be noted by the inspector's eye.

The man who ran the warehouse guaranteed this one thing—there was food of some variety in each can. He also claimed that nothing was spoiled, but, as he said, "For three cents what you gonna lose? You pay your money and take your choice."

Do you know how to tell the difference between peaches and plums by the shake of a can? Could you, by ear, distinguish carrots from corn? Well, your mother and I became well-nigh infallible as shakers of edibles.

Of course, no one is perfect; so, we sometimes drew chili for dessert. It sounds like fruit cocktail! Thank goodness, we had an icebox and plastic covers were cheap; so, we lived it up and laughed and ate away. In fact, it was great fun and we looked forward to our semi-monthly outing to the can hills.

For three dollars on payday we could purchase one hundred cans of nourishment, and the man was right—it was all palatable and all good! Sure, there were times when we wished we might be free of this small-change living and shop at the stores with the nice folks. But as we look back on it now, we list those days with our happiest memories.

The Bible says, "It is good for a man that he should bear the yoke in his youth." It also is good for a woman. And it is just about the finest for a man and a woman together if they are faced with the necessity of living largely on love for the first few years.

More important than the house you live in is what kind of you is living in the house!

How much the divan cost matters less than what you share there in visiting and dreaming and *innamorata!*

Your greatest need right now is not for a new stove, nor for new pots and pans, but for new fires to refine you and warm you and make your hearts glow. Though it may be hard to believe, you are fortunate indeed that your budget is limited.

Speaking of budgets, one of my favorite quotes on same is this from an unknown oracle, "A budget, strictly enforced, is like long underwear. If you need it, you better have it. If you don't, it scratches!"

You will probably learn that the man is right. You'll no doubt find it essential, and there will be times when it doesn't wear well. But here are some secrets to budgeting money which we have found invaluable.

Let's begin with first things first. At our house, as you know, we have lived by this money-motto:

"Give ten percent, save ten percent, and
spend the rest with thanksgiving and praise!"

We've never regretted that day when we made this decision. Some precepts, adopted early, make a mighty difference in the years to come.

That ten percent giving commitment is no place for faint hearts. When your first check comes in, you'll sit down and count up the bills, and you'll be tempted to join the "our-problem-is-different-from-everybody-else's" brigade.

You may rationalize. "When we get more, *then* we'll give more!" But you won't. This is one of those things where you either do or you don't.

It's your life to live, but you asked me to point you toward heaven on earth and, dollar-wise, this is "Gate One" to some wonderful discoveries.

Many people I see these days are desperately afraid. Some of these shivering souls are frightened by many things. But one of their major anxieties is that the good will be gone before they get their share.

It is true that some are clinging to fearsome memories out of their yesterdays. We must make allowance for their neuroses. But many couples would be richly blessed by a new philosophy of giving. They need to know that it is not enough to have "goods." These things are fleeting, but the secret to "the good life" is not in possessing more things.

The decision to give that ten percent first may also be your safety factor when the day of your prospering comes. You can't imagine it now, but the time will arrive when your money-pressures begin to let up. As this happens, some people start making their own rules. But if you have adopted certain basic principles in your lean years, you'll find that they act as safeguards when the fruits of your labor begin to ripen.

So, this is number one—Give ten percent and give it first!

Saving that second ten percent will also call for strict discipline. There are several reasons, however, why it is worth what it costs.

For one thing, it can prevent some of the foolish mistakes of overspending which we'll consider in our next letter.

Then, too, a mutually agreed savings program will give you the solid satisfaction of knowing that you are insuring your future. The stormy days will not catch you unprepared, nor will your son's education, nor that trip you need to broaden your horizons, nor even the wedding for your lovely daughter.

Operating on a definite principle can also free your mind to concentrate more clearly for better performance at your work. The time which you might waste in worry can now be dedicated to added efficiency which will guarantee an even more substantial base to your future.

Another merit which comes from saving a set percentage is that it might protect you against the dangers of over-saving. We see these poor souls too in the counseling room. They are victims of the poverty complex which compels them to hang on too tight to too much.

These folks assume that when they have more they'll be liberated to enjoy their accumulation. But they probably won't. Sometimes you can read it in their eyes—true joy is not to be found in stocks and bonds and bigger bank accounts. They are not sad because of their losses. Theirs is a money-melancholy which only increases as their gains increase.

It is a pitiful truth that *having* more sometimes leads to *being had!*

Let's close this one down with an observation on a familiar saying. It is often misquoted—"Money is the root of all evil!" But that is not how the original reads. Instead, it says "The *love of money*" is the origin of the error.

So now and then move your eyes from concentration on

the *intakes* and check to see if your *outlets* are in good order. The fact is that what goes from your pocket has a direct bearing on what comes in. This is a law of life.

In his original creation the Heavenly Father included certain of these unfailing principles. Out of his love he provided for the needs of all his children and he built his universe to meet these needs. When you observe his rules and live by them, he can tax the remotest sources to meet your every requirement.

I hope you will early learn this truth: If you keep your part of the covenant, you can never, ever outgive God!

Keep looking up,
Dad

WANT YOUR OWN WANTS

My dear Karen,

"*Make the very most of all you've got and make the very least of what you can't get yet!*"

This little jewel came from Grandma Davidson. I called her "the sage of Sugar Creek," which was my first student pastorate. Grandma had twenty-seven children and grandchildren. For Sunday dinner, it was some sight to sit with them at her table which originated in the dining room and extended to the far wall of her parlor.

Your mother and I were engaged, so I had my antenna out for guidance. While we leveled a mountain of fried chicken and asked for seconds on her homemade ice cream, my inner buzzers were getting the signal. These happy couples had what we wanted. They were very much alive to each other and at peace with their world.

124

I often stayed at Grandma's on my weekend visits. So one day I asked her to teach me what she taught her own "younguns," as she called them. Since she knew that her pastor friend was about to "be hitched" (quoting her again), she did what her Bible said—"She opened her mouth with wisdom."

Out of her numerous suggestions, I pass on to you here this brief item which I heard her say over and over—"Make the very most of all you've got and make the very least of what you can't get yet!"

It was clear that these solid unions of her sons and daughters were no accident. They had taken her words to heart, and one mark of their love was a rare quality which many couples miss. They had learned to enjoy their enjoyments and to deny their denials.

There are two facts which might apply to "loving that man" as we loiter a bit before this gem from Grandma Davidson's collection. One of these is particularly for feminine ears. The other may be something you and Vincent can use together.

1. *Give praise to your man and glory to God with loud "Thanks" and "Nice going" and "Hurrahs for you!"*

We've been at this door before in our letters. Whenever I seem to be taking you repeatedly down some well-beaten path you can be sure it's for one reason only. I've seen this so often that it bears repetition. In my work as a counselor I have come on too many women who believe they can "drive" their husbands to success with stern commands or subtle innuendos.

We both know that some men are laggards and their

laziness has an adverse effect on the whole family. But these are not our consideration here. I'm thinking rather of the host of earnest workers who are giving it their best and still can't satisfy that demanding woman at home.

Here are some statements from such ill-favored husbands to illustrate my point. The first is out of my own experience.

One day in my study I heard a worn-out husband make this tragic admission: "I've had it. It's an awful thing to say but I've got to say it. She's all right in her place, but her place hasn't been dug yet! I'm so desperate I'm even willing to give up the kids to get away from her pounding!"

The second comes from my reading. Heine, the German poet, is reported to have said that should he die before his wife he certainly hoped she would remarry in order that there might be one person in the world to regret his passing!

Read the first quote again and weep! Read the second once more and smile! But never, never allow yourself to employ that sinister smile which some women use to berate their husband's livelihood.

If you must make some changes, then do it intelligently together by honest discussion in love. Mix your phrases with praises for his best efforts and let him know your every word is for boosting him up and not for blowing him down.

Thanksgiving and gratitude are absolute musts for another reason which you may not have considered. Now and then a horrible thought skitters across nearly every male mind. If he is married and if he works, *he may feel trapped* when he's not up to his best. He once was free but now he must labor for his wife, for his children, and for those myriad spongy things at home which soak up his hard-earned dollars. When this is at its worst, he may even see his woman as a particular type of parasite. There she sits reading an interesting book, watching a soap opera, drinking coffee with the girls, while he slaves at the salt mines to make all this possible.

Fortunately, these are only flashes and, in part, this is somewhat impersonal. When he comes back to center he probably wouldn't even consider trading marriage to you for life on the loose again.

We have talked about warm words and warm gratitude and a warm body as an antidote for all this. There is still another mitigator you might keep in mind. *Let him have a healthy amount of say in how the money should be spent!*

There may be certain checks he likes to write. Or maybe he'll wish to handle them all. Unless he's a ruinous financier (some men are), he may prefer to preside over the funds while you admire over his shoulder. Especially during your early years, this "chancellor of the exchequer" role may be what his ego needs. If you laud him and boost his opinion of himself sufficiently, he may come home one day, as your father did, and say, "Honey, will you take over running the budget? I have so many important things to do!"

2. *Want your own wants!*

Some mathematical wizard has figured that the average modern family is exposed to another sales pitch 1,158 times daily. I don't know where nor how he gets his figures. But you know, when you stop to consider it, that all the adjectives of our language are harnessed to race the chariots of commerce and trade.

Turn on the radio, read the newspaper, flick on your television, read a magazine. Everywhere the swamis cry, "Lo, here! Lo, there! . . . Buy these! Buy them! Hurry, now, don't miss these bargains. . . . Be the first in your crowd to own one! Everybody who is anybody serves our brand. . . . You want to 'come up'? Then smoke our smokes. . . . Mother, father, sister, brother, you'll all smell swell with our deodorant! . . . Go this very minute to the cut-rate store! Pay your money for a bottle of these! . . . They're just right for what hurts you!" and, if nothing hurts, they're right for that, too!

The sharpies will get you if you don't watch out! They have a way of stealing the joy right out from under you. Their stuff is like dope. It's easy to get on but hard to get off. They'll try to convince you that what you make yourself can't possibly be as good as what they have made for you. With all the gusto of the old-time evangelist, they'll call you to glue your eyes on the new drapes, the new car, the new rug, or some other new item with an appalling appeal.

They'll even lend you the money to buy it and they make it so simple!—"Get your loan by mail!" And if you *have* fallen into the seller's traps there are other barkers to cry, "Now, wouldn't you like to consolidate your debts?"

When your mother and I were in school we borrowed from one of these "pay only us" places! I suppose it was not so, but it seemed that every month when we made our payments we owed a little bit more than the month before!

128

Be wary of borrowing at all, but, if you must, do it where the good guys are. If you aren't careful about this you may have innocently exchanged a few errors for a whole bunch. An anonymous poet puts it better than I could when he says:

> If a bank won't make the loan,
> Go without until they do.
> If it isn't good for them,
> It can't be good for you!

I see them often, these foolish people, who have clamored so greedily for "stuff" that they have overextended in their hysteria. Then, in their panic, they grasp for more and clutch so tightly to "things" that life's true values slip from their hands.

So, want your own wants! Don't let the "Buy, Buy, Buy" boys pilfer the pleasure of your present enjoyments! Make the very most of all you've got and make the very least of what you can't get yet!

Yea, yea and nay, nay!

HAPPY HOUSEKEEPING

My dear Karen,

        An old English proverb makes this claim: "There is but one hour a day between a good housewife and a bad one!"

Since my lifework is not housekeeping, I couldn't possibly have much to say of significance here.

But I do get into many homes, and I have observed some things which I offer humbly, realizing I am way over my head in this field.

1. *The good housewives I see seem to be organized.*

We teach the custodians at the church that they should clean these rooms Monday, that section on Tuesday, and especially make sure to tidy up the sanctuary on Saturday in preparation for Sunday's service. Maybe this English proverb carries its punch in the fact that it smacks heavy of system.

2. *The good housewives I see take pride in their homes.*

There are two extremes here and "right" must be somewhere in the middle. Some women make wrecks of themselves keeping a three-room apartment. It is not true that all female ulcers come from the big houses. As we've said before, most men grow weary of women who fuss and fume too much over details. I've seen some otherwise good marriages destroyed by perfectionist wives.

The opposite of this "a place for everything and everything in its place" female is no better. I was in a home the other day where we had to move great stacks of clothes to be ironed, magazines, ball gloves, brassieres, skates, and even a parakeet cage from chairs and divan before either one of us could sit down. Being a country boy, I also observed that they might have planted corn in the corners. The dirt was that thick.

With some things the blend is the thing, and I suspect that housekeeping is one of these. A sense of pride—but not too much! The casual life—but not too casual!

3. *The good housewives I see have somehow learned to make fun out of duty.*

Perhaps "pleasure" would be a better word than fun. Most men have no idea how much there is to housekeeping. They find out, of course, when something happens to mama for a time. It never occurs to most of us males that there are floors to wax, pans to clean, sheets to change, furniture to polish, diapers to wash, blouses to iron, towels to fold, and so on "seriatim and in extenso."

I, for one, am simply overjoyed that God made me a man. But some women seem to love it, they take pleasure in it, they make fun out of it.

As I was telling you, this is not my field and I better get out of it this very minute. But before I do here is another favorite proverb of mine. I keep this one also under the glass on my desk top.

"Most footprints on the sands of time were made with work shoes!"

Happy housekeeping,
Dad

A SAVORY SMELL
FROM THE KITCHEN

My dear Karen,

My commentary on cooking must have help from somewhere. You know I speak the truth. In the area of the oven and range my amateur standing has never been questioned.

Whenever your mother went to the hospital for bearing the latter members of our family offspring, I gave it my best. But my best was sadly lacking, and I can still hear the chorus-united, "Daddy, please, can't we go out for hamburgers tonight? *Please?*"

So, since we have under our roof one who "don't know from nothin'" (quoting your elder brother) and a true queen of the culinary arts, I asked the latter to give us a hand.

Then one day she presented me with what I think is a very nice thing. Here is your mother's alphabet for savory smells and meals at their best. In a few spots I've added a parenthesis.

"A" is for attractive service! Be alert to the beautiful colors in foods. Yellows and greens and reds and browns put carefully together can make your meals a thing of beauty.

"B" is for blessings at the meal! Notice I said *at* the meal! When your father was a boy he said that nobody dared take one bite until they had all "said grace" together. You know that many a piping-hot dish could be spoiled under this rigorous rule. So, we've always thanked God during our meals or afterward. We like it this way, and I have a feeling the Lord must like it too at our house!

"C" is to cook according to your budget! We learned in our married days at school that there are numberless ways to fix macaroni. Shopping can be a sporty game if you study the ads, spot the specials, and watch for the weekend bargains. You can do all this and still buy quality foods.

"D" stands for don't let him make his own breakfast! Especially for brides and mothers with children, it's "early to rise" for keeping your man in a mellow mood.

"E" is to eat by candlelight now and then! You know how happy the Brocks are. They tell us this is a regular event with them. Jim puts on his suit and tie. Joann

134

dresses in a lovely gown, and they sit by the fireplace with soft music, candles, and the children farmed out. They say it's one of the highlights at their house.

"F" is for festive occasions! We make the twenty-ninth of each month our "special" day because we were married that day in May. I know you'll remember our gala holiday dinners. I can hardly wait for the next one!

"G" is to go out together now and then! You will think that down in the future there will be plenty of time to live relaxed. This is a mirage. Tomorrow you will be busy, too. So budget some of your money for good times with each other alone.

"H" is to have your meals ready on time! Gadding about is part of the fun of being a woman. But never, never, never be about your gadding when you should be about getting your meals.

"I" is for imagination, a gift of the Lord. This is particularly good for what a famous eastern preacher refers to in his sermon, "Putting the Lure into the Leftovers."

"J" stands for joyful thoughts! In my home economics major we learned that digestion and attitudes are closely related. One of our psychiatrist friends points to "I'm fed up!" "You don't expect me to swallow that!" and "I can't stomach him!" to prove his claim that ulcers may come more from moods than from foods.

135

"K" is to kiss before the meal! You know one man who does this even in public. If there is one moment when I feel like a queen with the court looking on, this is the moment. And it also gives me a special little flutter at home.

"L" is for lingering when the meal is over! One time when your dad had taken you on an overnight trip to some speaking engagement, he came back with a lesson he's never forgotten. I guess you were ten or eleven and this is what he said, "For miles and miles we saw signs about 'The World's Deepest Well' in a small Kansas town. But when we came to it we simply couldn't stop if I was to make the banquet on time. Karen was quiet for some distance and then she said, 'Daddy, I feel sorry for you! You hurry so fast you miss the fun things!'" Right there he made the decision to slow down, and you did us all a big favor with that one.

"M" is for manners! "Thank you" and "No, thank you," "Please" and "Pardon me" make the meal nicer for everyone. This is in your domain and I'd see that the whole family knows, "This is not Sloppy-Joe's!"

"N" stands for nourishing foods! Have well-balanced meals for good health's sake!

"O" is to often prepare his favorite dishes! Learn how he likes them and serve them enough.

"P" is to plan ahead! It saves time and energy and fussing and fretting and headaches and money!

"Q" is for 'quainting yourself with the cookbooks! Learn to thank God there are people who know more than you do.

"R" is to remember the little things! Napkins and all the utensils, salt and pepper at both ends of the table, relishes, and flowers in a pretty vase are nice for some situations. (Never for ours. They get knocked over every time!)

"S" is for sharing with others! Let him bring his friends home. The children will also love you if they can invite theirs. Of course, you must train him and them to phone when delayed and let you know in advance. One of my friends thought she would "cure" her thoughtless husband forever when she heard by the grapevine that his boss was in town. She knew this was the night it would happen. So she threw on the bread and bologna, tossed on luncheon meat and lettuce, added tomatoes, mustard, and pickles. Guess what happened? The "visiting fireman" said it was the best meal he'd had in a week!

"T" is for television—turn it off! This goes also for radio and the news. (You know it requires a unanimous vote of our family to watch TV while we eat. There was one awful day which Peter and I will never forget. The Lions and Bears were playing their championship game. Someone voted "No!" I can't remember the culprit. This is another nice thing the Lord does for his children. As time passes, he dims our remembrance of who did what to whom.)

137

"U" stands for unexpected surprises! Someone describes one of the saints of yesterday with this charming line, "She always kept open for everyone the soul's east window of divine surprise." An extra-special menu which will tickle his taste buds, a classy dessert, or the exciting new recipe from one of your friends can work wonders.

"V" is for variety! We've said this several times, but it's easy to get in a rut. Experimenting is fun, so diversify for the good of all.

"W" is to welcome him warmly! This goes for when he comes home, when he comes to the table, when he comes with a problem, when he comes for love.

"X" stands for 'xtra helpings! Some need them. Some don't. Yet nobody likes stinginess. (A cute poem comes to mind. It's more about 'xtra pounds than 'xtra helpings, but I think you'll like it:

> "My girlfriend's waist is 42.
> She eats her meals in haste.
> And so, you see it's really true. . . .
> Haste makes waist!")

"Y" is for your own appearance! Grooming and cleanliness and fixing your pretty face to its very best are worth your attention.

"Z" is for zest! One of my good friends is fond of saying, "A warm meal can be ruined by a cold-hearted cook!"

Learn to enjoy your kitchen and fill it with love from your soul!

So, love that man and love him well from behind your stove. On a recent trip through the South we stopped at a little cafe in Kentucky. Above the door was a sign which read, "Something superior for your interior!" That's a fine goal for a housewife, too, isn't it?

Best wishes for a savory marriage,
Dad

IF ADVERSITY STRIKES

My dear Karen,

 The other day I was in a home where some well-wisher had done an attractive piece of needlepoint. It hung in an antique frame and the words of the woven motto were: "May there be just enough clouds in your sky to make a beautiful sunset!"

Very nice thought there, don't you think? But the reason I had come to this particular house was that the clouds were coming down now. The beautiful sunset had scattered, destruction was threatening, and the sky was getting darker all the time. There was bitterness and raging and life was rough, very rough!

The stern facts stood out bolder than the lovely thoughts in needlepoint. As I looked up there once more, I felt like stepping across the room to turn the motto to the wall. But I stayed where I was. We were hoping that the sun would return. Then the words would have meaning again and the sentiment would go nicely once more. Yet right now these hearts were moaning and their souls were bending low.

You know that like most parents we wish for you and Vincent a pleasant, peaceful life. The unknown poet puts well our prayer in his quaint line, "May the song of the dove be heard in your love and the small fowls make melody."

Yet, life is not always what we might prefer. Trouble in some form is a part of living for most people. There are a few who appear to have an inside track with the gods of good fortune. But for ordinary citizens there will be troubles and sickness, losses and woe, death and dilemma.

So what can you do if life gets hard? There are some things worth remembering. Suppose we call them "The A-B-C's for Adversity!"

A. One answer for these times is to *calmly face the fact that you will not be exempt from the harsh and troublesome.*

I would not purposely make you morbid, but you should know this: I see many foolish couples who go blindly along under the false assumption that a love such as theirs will be excused from bad luck and stormy weather. They mistakenly think that their license to marry included some guarantees for a life of ease.

You have taken a mature attitude toward all this when you say in unison: *"We seek a happy marriage with wholeness of heart, but we do not expect to reach the promised land without going through some wilderness together."*

141

B. A second help for the hard times is this natural follow-up of number one—*God does not promise his followers freedom from trouble.*

He only pledges that he will be with us when the thunder claps and the lightning flashes. I am glad you have learned the value of a vital religious faith.

We'll talk about this at length before we are done, but many people need nothing more than they need a new understanding of living continually with the Lord no matter what comes. Their idea of "being religious" is to attend church on Sunday. When they leave their places of worship, it is rather like giving God a wave of the hand and saying, "See you next week! Same time! Same place!"

One of my psychiatrist friends recently sent a troubled man to see me. When he called to make an appointment for his client he made this interesting statement, "I think we've cleared up most of his mental problems. He's a churchgoer and I think you might help him. What he needs now is someone who can help him find his answer eighteen inches lower down. He has it in his head. Now he needs it in his heart."

Praises be, this is not your problem. The wick of your lamp runs deep into the oil of the Eternal. You've been friends with the Lord for a long time and you know how to pray. You have learned that trouble does not mean God has gone off and left you. It does mean that he can use this for bringing you to higher ground if you will let him.

C. A third strengthening factor looms large as I go back over the case histories of marriages I have seen from the inside. This is that you do a big thing when you *determine*

142

together that the hard things will be used as sealers rather than dividers of your union.

Perhaps we can illustrate this by an amusing tale I heard from a rough old sheepherder friend of our Colorado days. He said that when a pack of fierce dogs plunder, or the coyotes come, there is one all-important difference between wild horses and wild asses. According to his account, when these deadly foes attack, the wild horses put their heads together in a tight center, tails to the windward side, and *proceed to kick the devil out of their adversaries.* But, if we can believe his reporting, when the wild asses are put upon, they place their heads toward the enemy, their tails to the inside, and *they kick the devil out of each other.*

I don't know whether he was "pulling my leg" as he loved to do. Yet his story does pack a wallop, doesn't it?

Particularly, I think it is a message for the married. I am sorry to report that most of the couples who come to my study remind me of the wild asses. They come kicking at each other, or at themselves, or at their marriage.

This is too bad. These husbands and wives have not learned their A-B-C's for handling adversity.

So, this is a good credo for a victorious union: "Why life is like this we do not know! But we know this! What happens is not so important as what we do with what happens. One day the sun will return and we will be better, finer people. God is never far away! Nothing shall separate us from togetherness with each other and with him."

Take courage,

Dad

SOMETIMES LOOK OUTWARD

My dear Karen,

True love of the highest kind is not gazing starry-eyed forever into each other's optics. In our last letter we talked about facing inward at the right time in the right way. But looking fondly toward each other is not the sole purpose of marriage.

So let's talk about keeping the windows of your home clear for an outward look. I recently heard a psychiatrist friend present an interesting paper on mental health. He said one thing which bears repeating. He told us that he advised one of his patients, "You should cut some windows in your selfishness. You must do this not only to let the sun in but to let your eyes look out. See the children playing. Notice the neighbor working his garden. Watch folks passing along the street. Count the cars as they go by.

This will be excellent therapy. You have forgotten that there are other people in the world besides yourself."

This physician of the mind touches here on one of the counselor's major problems. Some couples, as we have said, look too little at their mates. The major require-ment of others is a look inside themselves. Then, as the doctor says, there are those whose curative depends on looking outward together.

Here are some places where this applies.

Let's begin with *"friends."*

It is good for you and Vincent to be "best friends." Yet I have observed some marital friendships of the "me and thee" variety which started as a cozy little exclusiveness and never advanced beyond that. I hope you will learn to snuggle down into your environment. But don't let your environment snuggle down around you so much that you never share your warmth with friends.

Some of these selfish houses with the barred doors eventually become little more than nursing homes for a mutual narcissism.

So make friends and share your love because that's one of the big reasons why it was given you. Selfishness in any form is sin, and unless you work out the love which God has worked in, you may be a part of the world's evil rather than its blessing.

That you will choose your friends well we know by your history. In marriage certain friendships broaden insights; others are for laughs; and then there are those whose com-panionship is like a tree where you find shade.

There are also dangerous friendships which will gradually drain your sense of holiness unless you are alert to their fade-away influence. These are frequently in the "everybody-does-it" crowd. They are the "group-think" people who may drag you down into the moral sag of the times if you let them. With the gang where "everything goes," everything may be gone before someone has the courage to stand up and be different.

You never were a prig, and I'm sure you won't be two prigs strutting your piety together. But there is a vast difference between prudishness and true goodness born of inner conviction. Sometimes one couple's fortitude may be a blessing to others who only needed a leader. For some situations the sole solution is a clear "goodbye!" Whether you stand alone or turn up companions who were waiting for someone else to take the initiative is not important. What does matter is for you to continually remind yourselves that *you are here to transform the world and not to let the world transform you.*

Another outward move which needs consideration is the turn toward *relatives and in-laws.*

May your relationships with "the relations" be increasingly pleasant as the years pass. But some go in the opposite direction. Many people knock on the counsel room door for help with this.

Some of these originate when a husband or wife insists on perpetually burning incense to "dear old mom" or "good old dad." Others are nourishing bitter hatreds which can be easily understood considering the treatment they received.

I would wish that the fates might excuse you from this

problem. But if they do not there is one sure thing to re-member. Whenever you are tempted to put your own or your husband's kinfolk in their place, remind yourself again—with some folks it's what you don't say that counts!

Whatever the feeling, it is good to turn now and then toward the homes from which you came. If these rela-tionships are strained they usually are only more strained by staying away. "It's over the fields and through the woods to grandfather's house we go" may be a sentimental relic from the past. But you better believe this: You'll never have peace all the way to the center of your soul until you have worked out some kind of peace with brothers-in-law, sisters-in-law, parents-in-law, aunts, uncles, nephews, nieces, and the whole tribe. This *can* be accomplished, even if the only peace in this relationship is the peace in your own soul.

One more important outward swing of your doors bears the label, *social service.*

There is no community to which you could move, no open country where you might build your house, but that you have come into the zones of the unfortunate.

Some couples accept the pinched faces of the starved and forsaken as part of the scenery. Others look aghast and feel bad. Then they turn away to content themselves with feeling good because they felt bad.

Certain "vocal patriots" become armchair critics. Their chief targets are usually "the government" or "those folks" who are at least trying. This kind will propound their "wisdom (?) " as long as you listen. But their words are often only a substitute for action.

There are even mistaken saints who go to their prayer chambers to intercede on behalf of life's ill-favored. This is good, unless you make this your single contribution. God never accepts us on our knees if we should be standing up to some evil or moving out of our doors to blaze highways, cut channels, clear paths, and do what we can to extend the arm of mercy where it needs extension.

If you do adopt some worthy project as your challenge, you are in for discouragement. Often you will feel like crying, "What is *our* little effort against such odds?" Yet, if you give it a try and make an effort, you will discover another wellspring of satisfaction. This is the satisfaction which comes only to those who are dissatisfied enough to take up a post somewhere in the war against poverty, disease, and desolation.

William Allen White is purported to have said, "My advice to the garden clubs of our land is to raise more hell and fewer dahlias." Some of the advance guard of the human race have been "hell-raisers" for "heaven's sake."

Perhaps you will be moved to join a "community cause." Or you may feel an inner compulsion to declare yourself against some gaping wrong which you see clearly as an insult to society. Now your comfort and safety-first must give way to speaking out, even if you are misunderstood. Great things have been started by solo voices when there was no other voice to join them.

It is important that you check now and then to be sure you are not swept up in "good causes" to the neglect of some basic assignments with a prior claim. You will like this story of the weary husband who brought his wife down to earth one night with a thud. She arrived home late from her political rally, plopped herself in the big chair, kicked off her shoes, and announced, "It was great, Henry! We're going to sweep the state!" Poor Henry who had done the dishes, put the children to bed, and struggled with the vacuum cleaner, listened her through. Then he came with this caustic comment, "Sounds great! Why don't you start with the living room?"

The tricky business of doing right for wrong reasons also needs checking now and then. Some reformers are merely blowing a neurotic foghorn out of a crack in their emotional structure. This is not good. The world needs only the clearest trumpets for social righteousness. The "slightly sick" doers of good may accomplish some things worthwhile, but they might also undermine what the healthy are building.

Sometimes in the church we see these "brothers and sisters of good causes" running about, mopping feverish brows, convinced that fate has assigned them to attend single-handed to the salvation of all. One mark of mental well-being in social service is to remember that you are not expected to clean up the whole earth.

You get the message. There are two common maladies here. One is the sickness of crusading in places meant for other reformers. The second is to close our doors to the trumpet sounds which *were* meant for our ears.

The growing "let's-don't-get-involved" philosophy is not for people with your abilities. "Under the Spreading Apathy" is more than a clever title for a book. This is a real threat to the nation. When too many nice folks become indifferent, the next step is likely to be indifference to the indifference, and this may be a sign that the end is approaching. Always one telltale mark of decay is the assumption that we are good merely because we have refrained from being bad.

So, if yours is a healthy marriage, you will be looking out, moving out, crying out some of the time. But, for goodness' sake, be constantly checking your motives.

The main motive, of course, is traceable to your very reason for living. In another letter we'll give further thought to the fact that you were not put here on earth, nor put into each other's arms, to serve only yourselves.

It is a startling realization when any couple faces this truth: *There is something more important in the world than our own happiness!*

I hope you will know the thrill which comes to those who leave the place better than they found it.

Think big,
Dad

WHEN NOTHING WORKS

My dear Karen,

Not for a moment would I attempt to convince you that all good wives have good husbands. It simply is not so.

Generally, it is true that you get what you pay for. But some souls pay the full price and receive no recompense. There are men who turn out to be bad matches for even the finest women. She may give him her all; he takes everything and gives her nothing.

There is no more desolate sight than a brokenhearted woman who put her whole soul into her marriage and got back only a heart full of broken dreams.

They say that life is ten percent what you make it and ninety percent how you take it. That is a very clever statement but, like many such, it doesn't cover the entire radius. I have seen some of the Lord's ladies who went ninety percent of the way, or even ninety-nine, and their reward was an absolute blank.

Of course, all this really has nothing to do with you and Vincent. We *know* your marriage will be a resounding success.

Yet, I did want to write this one letter to ask you to reserve a very special kindness for those who are not so fortunate. They need the tenderest touch your hand can give. They need a ready ear and a sincere friend to share their tears. So whenever this happens in the vicinity of your heart, make haste to open your soul with godly sympathy. You will also want to open your lips in a prayer for a better tomorrow than their shattered yesterdays have been.

The happier you are the more you must stretch out room inside yourself for those who have not found life so good and beautiful as you have found it.

Ten little letters make up a great word:

"Compassion!"

Yours for a compassionate heart,

Dad

GREATER THAN
THE TWO OF YOU

My dear Karen,

"I worship you!"—"You're an angel!"—
"Our love is heavenly!"—these are welcome sounds to
lovers' ears.

But be sure you understand them in their proper con-
text.

Self-reverence may be good, and two selves in reverence
for each other might be even better. But this might also
be sick, very sick, unless this reverence is part of a larger
reverence.

You will remember from your science courses that it
is the sun which keeps the solar system from flying apart.
The world and everything in it, including you and Vincent, would come undone if it were not for this magnetic
force holding things together.

This is how it is with marriage. Two may be born in opposite hemispheres, or they may have grown up in the same block, but what matters most is this—*are they being held together at the center by a holy love which is stronger than their own?*

This is the basic question because of one inescapable fact. Even the most "divine" creature on earth has one thing in common with the rest of the populace—we are all human!

At our present stage of development, one bit of standard equipment on homo sapiens is an innate tendency to selfishness.

Whether it was the amoeba in the swamp or the first creature on legs or the ape swinging from his tree or some shaggy-haired ancestor with club in hand, or whoever is to blame—the truth is that most of us have not evolved far enough to be free of this instinct to self-preservation.

"Look out for number one!"—"I want what I want when I want it!"—"Me first, me second, me third!"—these are villains waiting in the wings of any marriage when the lover's song has died away.

You may determine that you *will* think of the other fellow first. You *will* try to see life through his eyes. You *will* be sweet and gentle and kind this whole day long. But, if you are like your dad, within thirty minutes this noble vow is one more beautiful theory murdered by a gang of brutal facts.

So where do we go from this dilemma?

The answer, as I have learned it at our house and observed it times without number in counseling with others, is the theme of this letter.

Here is *the key of keys* to love at its radiant best: *That couple who understands that their union is for Someone greater' than the two of them has discovered the secret gate to marriage at its best.*

Let's take a look now at how you can bring your lives together to this blessed estate.

Recently, I heard some mathematically minded minister on the radio make these interesting claims. He cited the fact that one marriage in four ends in divorce. He said that for families who attend church regularly, the rate of broken homes is one in fifty-four. He further stated that for families who pray together, the ratio is one to five hundred.

He didn't say where he got his figures, but after hearing his testimony I made an analysis of my own experience.

My record looks like this. In twenty years I estimate that I have counseled with more than two thousand couples who came to me with their problems. This includes husbands, wives, or both of them together. Their problems ranged from triviality to tumult.

Now hear this! *I have never had one couple or one member of a marriage come to me with their troubles if they prayed together.* (There were a few, perhaps a dozen, who said, "We used to!")

So, this is my witness. One out of so many visits the clinics. One of this many is severed in the courts. But in my own experience, *one out of none* was broken beyond repair if they had slipped their joined hands into the hand of God through prayer.

Let me list for you here the prayer steps which I have recommended to hundreds of couples:

1. Make a compact that you will set aside some time each day when you look Godward together.

2. Select some devotional guide which suits you. There are many of these in the bookstores, and most churches have them on their literature racks.

3. When your appointed time has come, you sit together quietly while one of you reads the day's selection.

4. Now you talk over what you would like to pray about. If Vincent is concerned with something in his business, he may appreciate an opportunity to tell you this. Perhaps you will confess that he hurt your feelings this morning and you haven't been able to put that where it belongs. You may ask for clarification, if you need it, but you will not argue. You simply place before each other the things which are on your hearts.

5. Then you hold hands, bow your heads, and pray silently to God as you understand him. It will probably be best if you do not begin by praying out loud together. Unless you have done this frequently, it may be so awkward and embarrassing that you won't keep it up after the first few attempts.

6. When you feel that you have "gotten through," you pray the Lord's Prayer together.

As you develop this art between you there will be times when your prayer will major in silent listening. Gradually, your perception enlarges until you understand that prayer is not for your getting what you want from God. It is for him getting what he wants from you.

You will also begin to comprehend that prayer is not searching, nor begging, nor pleading. It is rather opening up to the God who is already knocking at your heart door. This opening of doors, conscious doors and subconscious, is prayer at its very best. You make a great discovery when you sense that the first move of the divine-human encounter is God's move. He is constantly seeking lives where he can enter to glorify the earth with his love.

Learning to pray together takes time, as all good things in marriage take time. But it does make sense, doesn't it? God is love and you both believe he is the author of your union. So the more you create channels through which his divine love can flow into your human love, the greater your love will be.

It is important that you learn this and practice it together. It may be dangerous for one person to stand still while the other advances. Wedlock is not for widening the distance between two people. It is for closing gaps in their differences until these two separate lives cohere around a Holy Center which is life as it was meant to be.

What I am saying here is not mere theory. Time and again I have seen marriages which seemed utterly hopeless come to a newness of life through the practice of silent prayer together.

But I am speaking also from personal experience. It was a big job your mother took on when she walked down the aisle to take this hand and hear the preacher say, "Dearly beloved, we are assembled here to join this man and this woman in holy wedlock."

It was not long until she discovered that there were many warring selves she must bring together in this boy she had taken to raise. Her challenge was to draw a rough, scarred, and woolly male into oneness with her inner calm, her softness, and her gentle femininity.

But you know how she did it, don't you? I watched her sitting there in the early morning with her Bible and her books. She called it her "quiet time," and I came to understand that her serenity of soul was the answer to my confusion.

Then one day in my desperation I asked her to lead me, too, "beside the still waters." So she took me with her to her school of prayer, and that's how I know firsthand that this is the key of keys.

Today, after twenty-six years of marriage, I am more sensitive to the thrill of her presence than I have ever been. When I come on her unexpectedly in a crowd, it is like a glad little song rising up somewhere inside me. When I catch her eye in public, it is as though she were hanging out a sign with the exact word of inspiration I need right then. When I drive home in the evening, I must consciously guard the foot pedal lest I step on the gas a bit too fast as I approach the house where she waits for me. I still count it the day's biggest thrill when she comes hurrying from wherever she is to greet me with a holy kiss and press her body close against mine in yearning. And as I look down the road ahead, I see an elderly man and woman going into the sunset hand-in-hand. I know in my heart that the end will be better by far than the beginning.

I could wish for Vincent no greater gift than this—that

his wife might lead him, as her mother led her dad, to the secret chamber of divine communion where two lives are blended into a sacred trinity.

I hear some of the sociologists arguing that one solution to the marital breakdown of our times is to make divorce harder. That could help in some cases, but the real answer is not to make divorce harder. It is to make marriage what it should be. And what it should be is a sacred triune relationship between the Lord and you and your husband forever and ever.

Prayerfully,
Dad

She was pure joy and she could only create unhappiness by being absent!

(An anonymous tribute to a saint of the gentler gender.)